The Athena Principles

Simple Wellness Practices
for Overworked Professionals

The Athena Principles

Simple Wellness Practices
for Overworked Professionals

by Kathy Robinson

June 2021

COLLABRIA
PUBLISHING

Published by: Collabria Publishing
Cover and Book Design by: Liz Kalloch Design and Illustration

ISBN:
Library of Congress Control Number:

*Dedicated to my maternal lineage, who paved the way
for me to have choice and give voice in ways they could not.*

*And with love and gratitude to Christina Baldwin,
whose Circle of Storycatchers forever changed my heart
and the trajectory of my life.*

contents

preface

I noticed an interesting phenomenon as I was getting ready to leave my corporate life. My colleagues were curious as to what would follow a 33-year career, with guesses ranging from moving to a warmer climate to enjoying a gap year.

When I shared that I had studied to become a certified wellness coach and was writing a book about wellness for professionals, the conversation inevitably changed. There was a glance to see if anyone was around, a lowering of the voice, and then the conversational floodgate would open.

Some had recently switched to a plant-based diet, some had started a meditation practice, some were training for an athletic event for the first time in their lives, some were interested in energy work, some longed to leave their current job, and some just wanted to carve out some space for themselves in their ever-busy lives.

I walked away from those conversations happy that my colleagues were open to making positive changes, but saddened that their wellness intentions had been kept quiet until they felt safe enough to have such a conversation. Then I remembered that when I began to make positive changes, such as developing my own meditation practice, it wasn't a topic of discussion with my work colleagues either.

These conversations led me to sharpen the focus of my consulting business: my goal became helping busy executives implement simple wellness practices (what they do) to optimize their well-being (how they feel), especially during times of transition or when striving toward new wellness goals. It's my aspiration to help professionals reignite their connection to their authentic selves and, in turn, become more productive in the workplace and more engaged at home and in their community.

Living and leading authentically – being seen for who we are – has gotten a lot of press in the business world. But there are still times and places where being yourself may not feel safe or may be feared as potentially detrimental to a career.

But as I learned during the conversations with my now ex-coworkers, the business community is yearning for genuine, connective communication. It's my hope that this book will help facilitate these meaningful conversations – with ourselves, our loved ones and our colleagues.

Kathy Robinson
May 2020
www.AthenaWellness.com

introduction

When I was 54 years old, I crossed a finish line that would have seemed impossible and unimaginable when I was 20 years younger.

I had been running a mile-long course loop in northern New Jersey for more than five hours when the official signaled I was starting my final lap. A few hundred yards later, I passed a parked car where my friends were camped out, shielding themselves from the relentless November wind and cold, leaping out to hold up handcrafted signs that read, "We're proud of you, Ninja Momma!" my nickname at the gym. It was uplifting to hear them cheer each time I had passed them since mile 26.

"This is it!" I yelled, raising my arms as I ran past, feeling a surge from the adrenaline rush. "Meet you at the finish line!"

I came to an exposed corner of the route where the wind had raged all morning and once again, the gust pounded my chest like an ocean wave, my arms and legs working hard with little to show for it. The jolt shot down my hamstrings, which had tightened each lap since mile 20. The back of my body felt like it was in a vice grip.

But as I neared the finish line, I barely felt my body. I grinned as I saw my friends capturing the moment on their phones while urging me on. I raised my arms in a V, Rocky style, and pumped my fists yelling "Yes!" as I surged across the finish line. I ran into their arms and jumped up and down in celebration.

I had just finished my first 50k ultramarathon.

Twenty years prior, I couldn't run one lap around a track.

Just five years out of my 20s, I felt like a middle-aged woman due to stress and poor lifestyle choices. I was a year into a new corporate job I did not like that was accompanied by a long daily commute. I was eating the wrong foods, not moving my body and giving little attention to sleep.

In response to these stressors, I drank liberally and kept a relentless schedule of parties, concerts and never-ending activities with my partner, family and friends. As a result, I had gained 25 pounds in the 13 years since college graduation.

In rare quiet moments, I would acknowledge I needed to make some lifestyle shifts, but I was never sure how to go about it.

One day at work, I noticed a colleague in the coffee room shaking a plastic tumbler and asked what he was doing. He said he was following a new workout and eating routine that included protein shakes, a new concept at the time.

At lunchtime I walked over to Barnes & Noble and bought the book about the program he was following, *Body for Life* by Bill Phillips. It was full of before-and-after pictures. I was intrigued. While I was impressed with the after pictures, I could not imagine taking a picture of myself in a bathing suit. But there was something about the simplicity of the *Body for Life* program that gave me hope. I started changing my lifestyle in earnest.

The workouts consisted of cardio and weightlifting components. I bought a treadmill and put it right next to my bed and borrowed a weight bench and some weights and put those next to the treadmill. Clothes were laid out the night before and I exercised first thing in the morning. I made working out unavoidable.

To ensure I was able to follow the nutrition part of the program, I emptied the fridge and cupboards and filled them only with the foods listed in the book – vegetables, lean proteins and healthy fats.

Each week, there were three simple weightlifting routines that rotated between upper and lower body workouts. Three cardio days were interspersed with the strength workouts that consisted of 20-minute laddered intervals. Sunday was a rest day.

Since I was unable to run for any length of time, my cardio intervals consisted of walking for one minute at 3 mph (20-minute mile), then 3.3, 3.5, 3.7 culminating with a one-minute jog at 4 mph (15-minute mile) before catching my breath for the next set. I came face-to-face with the fact that I was overweight and out of shape in my mid-thirties.

Worlds away from the track and cross-country running I did in high school, the endurance I once enjoyed was long gone. I felt the extra weight I carried with each step. I was shocked that I had allowed myself to get so out of touch with my body.

Thankfully, consistency brought progress. I completed the workouts as best I could each day. About six weeks into the program, a colleague asked what I was doing differently, commenting on my weight loss. I was feeling good, too, and my clothes were fitting better, which I guess was evident.

The program mechanics of strength and cardio routines coupled with simple clean eating changed my body. But something else happened when I started working out and focusing on my diet – I began showing up for myself.

This meant being willing to acknowledge where I was in my life, getting in touch with what mattered to me, and taking positive steps toward that vision. This set me on a path from a sedentary life to an active one – toward a lifetime of learning how to continuously increase my wellness level beyond the physical to include mental, emotional and spiritual well-being.

I was lucky. My wellness wake-up call was more of a realization than a crisis, and I was able to make deliberate changes over time. This was the first of three wellness realizations I would have over a ten-year period. This first one was focused on exercise and nutrition, which prepared me to go deeper with subsequent realizations into other areas such as meditation and creativity that would further enhance my overall well-being.

For many people, the need to focus on health may be more immediate through a diagnosis or a test result. Conversely, the call toward wellness may feel vague, like more of an elusive pull to incorporate healthier and more meaningful life choices.

Whatever the reason, my guess is you're holding this book because you're looking to make some sort of positive change in your wellness profile, perhaps beyond diet and exercise.

The ability to run my first endurance race at age 54 is the byproduct of more than 20 years of learning and experimenting, but it wasn't the original goal. Although I didn't realize it at the time, I was longing for more than just a change from the sleepless nights, stressful days, and alcohol-filled weekends that were taking a toll on my body. I was longing for a connection to myself.

By the time I turned 40, it looked as if I had it all together. I had lost 25 pounds and kept it off, was hitting the gym regularly, had a loving partner and family, and worked for a top tier Wall Street firm. But on the inside, I was barely hanging on.

Due to an organizational change, I was working for a new boss who was not a fan of mine. The feeling was mutual. I was assigned new responsibilities and created a new team in this unstable environment. I never knew when the priorities would shift and he routinely called out my peers publicly when they weren't performing to his expectations.

I dug in. Not willing to be one of his scapegoats, I overdelivered on every single priority. In this unspoken chess game, the king would see these small successes and pile on more assignments. In response, the pawn – me – would add more hours to the work week by staying late at night, taking calls from the Asia team late on Friday nights and meeting with the European team early on Monday mornings. The weekends brought a little relief because catch-up work could be done in the comfort of my own home.

The stress compounded as the months passed. I would wake in the morning with a start, nauseous from the adrenaline already pumping through my body. Due to the late nights at the office, it wasn't unusual for me to get only four or five hours of sleep. Well aware of the full day that awaited, I would pull myself out of bed to begin the morning routine that would get me on the road by 6:30 a.m.

The commute into New York City was the nicest part of the day, as I shared the driving with my partner and it was the only time we got to catch up during the work week. We would note the changing seasons during the drive along the West Side Highway that bordered the Hudson River.

"I knew I was teetering on the edge of dis-ease, given the pressure I was under. Eating well and working out were my release valves."

The first sign of spring was the blooming of crocuses in Riverside Park, which runs from Harlem to the Upper West Side along the highway. The approach of summer was announced by the appearance of sailboats in the Hudson at the 79th Street boat basin marina. The West Side turned golden in the autumn and the boats were stored for winter, when the commute to and from work would be made in the dark. The rest of my work days were spent in a sterile, temperature-controlled office.

Besides the daily connection with my partner, the other non-negotiables in my life were diet and exercise. I knew I was teetering on the edge of dis-ease, given the pressure I was under. Eating well and working out were my release valves.

My partner was a huge support in those days. She had a manageable work schedule and while she would share the ride into the city with me, she would take public transportation home when her day was done. She prepared healthy food for us to take to work, which is where I ate most of my meals.

Back then, my goal was to work out four times a week. I had flexibility on Saturdays and Sundays. But twice a week, I would do all I could to leave the office by eight p.m., changing into my workout clothes before I got into my car to drive straight to the gym in New Jersey. If I made it there by nine o'clock, I would have an hour to exercise before the facility closed at ten.

I can remember some nights, sitting in my car in the parking lot of that gym, feeling foggy and buzzy from the exhaustion and copious amounts of caffeine consumed during the day. I couldn't bear to think about getting on the treadmill or lifting a weight. I would bargain with myself, "Just go inside and begin. You don't have to do the full workout."

Of course, once I got moving and the blood started flowing, I would feel the connection with my body, with something other than the all-consuming pressure cooker I worked in. That connection was an important reminder that there was more. It was like a faint whisper that something needed to change.

After eighteen months, I made an unexpected chess move. I knew I was in desperate need of some time off and a change of scenery.

I devised a plan that would allow me to take my unused vacation time so my partner and I could drive our camper van to Alaska via the Alaska highway, a trip that was on both of our bucket lists. This was in the days before continuous cellphone service blanketed the globe, so I rented a satellite phone in case of emergency and bought a phone card to check my work voicemail once a day. I instructed my team to leave a voice message should I be needed.

The pawn didn't ask the king if she could go.

I told my boss when I was leaving and when I'd be back – a total of 25 days counting weekends and holidays – an unprecedented amount of continuous time off. I was well aware this was a career-limiting move.

At that time, it was the first leap of faith I had ever taken in my corporate career. I had no plan beyond the road trip and I instinctively knew this break from the norm would not sit well with my boss. Nevertheless, we were Alaska-bound. The trip would prove to be the catalyst for the second phase of my wellness journey.

Although it took almost two weeks on the road before I could unwind, the combination of driving 10,000 miles and spending time in unfettered wilderness began to work its magic, alchemizing the raw experience of the last eighteen months at work into some semblance of meaning.

The mental processing was helped by the fact that I was getting to do all the things I had forgotten I loved. I took pictures, shot video, wrote, drove, listened to music, spent time in nature, spent time with my partner and enjoyed what I called "road movies" – watching the passing landscape of towns and fields and countryside through the windshield of the moving van while listening to my favorite playlists.

At the beginning of week three of the trip, while zigzagging on unpaved roads in the Alaska Boundary Range, I had a moment of clarity. I felt something shift and knew I needed to make some changes when I got back.

I realized my past habits had created an unbalanced state of wellness – all the things I loved, from my partner to writing to spiritual discovery, were cordoned off from my professional life. To create a healthier future, I needed to change my habits and focus on spending more time doing what I loved and find ways to bring more of my emotional, creative and spiritual sides into my daily life.

Within weeks of returning to work, I got a call from a former boss I had loved working with a number of years back. He had moved to a company in New Jersey and asked if I'd be interested in joining his team. I resigned within three months of my return from Alaska.

Pawn attacked king – checkmate.

Looking back, the act of defining what gave my life meaning became a tipping point for that lifestyle change, and my wellness choices began to better align with my desires and values. As a result, it became easier to identify what the right choices were for me and then follow through. I finally stopped working against myself.

For example, when I started my new job, I had time in the morning to work out and made sure to be home most nights by seven. This opened time for my partner, writing, reading, and preparing for the next day before getting to bed at a reasonable hour.

These changes didn't happen overnight. At the time, each step didn't feel like it was part of a longer journey or that it was leading to a more energetic, purpose-driven life. I could see none of those things as the years unfolded. In fact, it felt unremarkable day after day. But the results were cumulative and the small steps I took to pursue things I loved had a big and lasting impact over time. In the process, I became a woman who redefined midlife well-being for herself by learning to be self-compassionate and making space for the activities that fed her mind, body and spirit.

You, too, can transform your life by taking small steps and reprioritizing your wellness. You don't need a big goal, like an ultramarathon or job change, to experience greater vitality. Having the energy to flow through the day or the functional strength to work around the house without feeling depleted is a great place to start. You may, as I did, find yourself going deeper into the process as you experience initial positive results.

Whatever your aspiration, *The Athena Principles* will help you make positive wellness changes in a way that feels right for you.

What's the significance of Athena?

Athena was the Greek goddess of reason, intellect and art. According to Greek mythology, she was born fully grown, springing from the forehead of her father, Zeus. Known for being fierce and brave in battle, she was also principled, only engaging in war when it was in defense of state or home.

While Athena carried a spear and shield to signify strength, she was also considered the most intelligent and wisest of the Greek gods. She was said to be a savvy strategist and innovator and often pictured with an owl on her shoulder depicting her wisdom and near an olive tree, a symbol of peace and hope. She was a patron of the arts and, according to some sources, known for her generosity and compassion, as well as her ability to give courage to those in need of that trait.

For me, Athena represents the perfect balance between left-brain logic and objectivity and right-brain intuition and creativity. She was independent, unapologetically herself, and fully owned her power.

Are there times when attending to your responsibilities requires the strength and wisdom of a Greek goddess? Do you feel like you're living disparate inner and outer lives? Do you wish you could tap into and rely upon your inner knowing?

You may be called upon to run a household, manage your career, care for elders, and see to the needs of your partner and family. Somewhere in the execution and busyness, your own needs and desires can get buried until you lose touch with yourself.

Midlife brings the opportunity to examine where and how your time is spent and the freedom to say no to the things that don't align with what you value most. Another offering of midlife is the willingness and ability to be open to honest self-questioning. This, in turn, can lead to reshaping your current life into an integrated one that flows with vitality, creativity and connection. This process can be nothing less than transformative.

You will find that big leaps of effort are not required to make impactful change. Rather, this transformation is a quiet revolution that starts deep within, unnoticeable to others at first.

Taking small actions and consistently reinforcing them with a positive outlook will help you live more authentically, making you strong, confident and unstoppable. Best of all, this approach to integrate your inner and outer worlds and incorporate principled practices into your life can be personalized.

The philosophy behind *The Athena Principles* is "one size fits one" – an adage I learned when working with a consultant in my risk management days. This is your journey, your path, your way. There is no one right approach to enhanced well-being, only the right approach for you.

While the framework and Principles have wide applicability, the tools can be customized and the methodology is flexible to fit your unique experience. In other words, each step can be adapted to meet your needs.

This book is an invitation to reimagine the midlife experience. It outlines a holistic, integrated approach to create a lifestyle of principled practices and actions that will help you discover and reprioritize yourself, and to align who you are in the world with your deepest self.

The first section of the book will help you understand the important link between self-integration and health and how to build a strong body, calm mind and enlivened spirit. We'll review *The Athena Principles* framework and methodology and learn simple writing practices designed for non-writers as a means to connect with our inner selves.

The second section will include an in-depth look at the five Principles and include related exercises designed to:

- Cultivate self-compassion and self-acceptance (*Principle 1*)

- Use intention to clarify your heart-based "Why" behind transformation (*Principle 2*)

- Stay committed, consistent and engaged in the process (*Principle 3*)

- Implement a growth mindset as an accelerator (*Principle 4*)

- Create an ongoing feedback loop of modification and celebration (*Principle 5*)

- Develop nurturing morning and evening routines and an ongoing learning process to support your transformation.

Together we'll explore the barriers that have kept you from realizing the best version of yourself, and find ways to tap into your inner knowing in a way that will reshape your life.

Just like Athena, you already have the strength and wisdom for the journey ahead. Let's get started!

wholehearted living

Hanna is a 51-year-old banker who has balanced a successful career with her home life for decades. On most mornings when the alarm sounds, she swats it to snooze mode for ten more minutes of sleep. After it buzzes again, the smell of coffee pulls her out of bed for the promised boost of caffeine.

Her morning routine can be chaotic, especially if there's an unexpected schedule change. It can be a sprint to get her husband and teenage son on their way and she sometimes skips breakfast to get ready for work. Most days as she heads out the door, she steps over the duffle bag half-packed with workout clothes because there is no time to go to the gym.

Hanna typically takes calls during the commute to the office when she's not traveling. Whether in the office or on the road, her work days are filled with back-to-back meetings.

In the evening, her routine is much like the morning. After playing catch-up with her family and replying to urgent work emails, she numbs out with some television and maybe a glass of wine or two before dropping into bed later than anticipated.

When she finally turns off the light to try to sleep, her mind is still racing through the day's events. She feels guilty because she knows what she should be doing to take better care of herself, but she's not taking time to eat better or exercise.

Hanna is more troubled by how unseen she feels on this treadmill of activity and wonders how to make time for herself in her days of never-ending busyness. She thinks of the things that used to bring her joy, like gardening and photography, activities she hasn't done in years.

Hanna understands that she's functioning, but as her stress levels rise and she further disconnects from herself, she also knows she's not really living. How can she get herself back on track?

A few years back I was in the audience listening to the poet David Whyte recall a story from the days before he dedicated himself to poetry full-time. He was working at a non-profit organization and was experiencing high levels of stress and exhaustion.

When a friend, who was a Benedictine monk, came to visit him one evening, David started the conversation by seeking advice, "Tell me about exhaustion," he said.

The monk replied, "You know, the antidote to exhaustion is not necessarily rest. The antidote to exhaustion is wholeheartedness. You're so exhausted because you can't be wholehearted at what you're doing... because your real conversation with life is through poetry."

Using this story as an example, David suggested that we ask ourselves what we most care about in our lives. He reminded us that this is a conversation we delay having even though knowing what we're wholehearted about is a necessity, not a luxury. The more time passes, the more difficult it is to delve into what we care most about in our work, life and heart.

Like Hanna, and many of my clients, colleagues and friends, wholehearted living is elusive. Having a meaningful conversation with ourselves about what we care about most is something that is easily postponed or reprioritized.

Perhaps you, too, can relate to the feeling of separation between who you are in the outer world and how you feel inside. It can manifest as feeling off-track, scattered, or not fully engaged in life – as if your true self is not being fed.

How does this separation occur?

As we mature, we define ourselves through values, beliefs and the roles we play, including partner, employee, parent, relative, community member and friend. In addition, expectations of loved ones, employers or society in general may not align with how we feel inside or what value we place on that which is important to us. The disconnect widens when we do not see our true self reflected in our outer world.

The disassociation from self leaves us vulnerable to unhealthy habits that temporarily relieve the uncomfortable feeling of not being oneself in the world. In addition, we may feel a fear of rejection when we don't behave in accordance with the desires of others. This can lead to shame and hiding from our truth.

Such disconnect can be fueled and numbed by many things, including routine, activity, controlled substances, alcohol, food, social media or inertia. The disconnect may also manifest in the need to prove one's worth through overachievement or striving for perfectionism, sacrificing one's mental, emotional and physical needs for acknowledgement or acceptance. All of this can be further compounded by the stress of living someone else's beliefs and values as well as the energy it takes to protect the unspoken and unexpressed selves in order to fit in – in other words, to live a double, inauthentic life.

The good news is that although our true self may be buried or withered, it never goes away. There are wellness practices that can help us identify, acknowledge and address the disconnect. Through trial and error, we can reclaim our lives by identifying what's truly important to us and making choices that align accordingly.

What are the qualities of fully aligned, wholehearted living? It's the knowledge and expression of our true self without the need for outside validation or adjusting to other's expectations. It's a feeling of worthiness, of knowing you are enough. It's the practice of living honestly and setting healthy boundaries, including time for self-care. It's when our words and actions are congruent with our own beliefs and values.

"What are the qualities of fully aligned, wholehearted living? It's when our words and actions are congruent with our own beliefs and values."

In order to live in this manner, we need to find ways to connect and understand what beliefs and values are truly ours and identify what we're carrying from the past, including our own insecurities. It's not unusual to feel the emergence of a rebellious second adolescence in midlife as a means of finding out who we really are coupled with an urgency when we realize there is less time to postpone releasing any false personas.

Discovering your true self isn't a one-and-done exercise nor is there a switch that can be flipped to begin living from our authentic self. As the process begins to unfold, we are still required to perform in the roles and structures we created decades ago. We still need to be a partner, earn a living, parent our children, and participate in family and community activities – all while rediscovering what matters most to us apart from these roles and our outward identity.

It can be a one-step-forward-two-steps-back process, as the tension builds between our old and new emerging selves. It takes vigilance to defend against negative, outdated self-talk tracks, challenge outdated beliefs and examine our insecurities – all of which can creep back and try to sabotage our new patterns and habits.

Taking the time to reconnect with herself was the hardest part for Hanna. As she started to examine her old thought and behavior patterns and implement small changes, she felt pulled back to her old ways by habit, routine and the expectations of her family.

She needed a safe space for exploration, to recreate her narrative in a way that made emotional sense. A place to have the time to reflect on what resonated and felt true for her at this stage of her life. A place to evaluate new ideas and different ways of living and being. A place to answer the question – am I living my life or someone else's?

She created this space by developing a simple writing practice. She bought a small notebook she could carry with her throughout her day and filled it with bullet points and brief reflections. This helped her begin to understand her inner landscape. She also used her phone to capture images that moved her as well as self-portraits to visually express the way she was feeling. She even used the voice memo feature to capture insights on the go.

Hanna began to get a sense of what wholeness could feel like as she explored areas that were important to her. Instead of adding to her overloaded schedule during the week, Hanna began to focus on the things she could stop doing that would positively impact her well-being. She decided on a 90-day No Alcohol Challenge and began experimenting with intermittent fasting to naturally increase her energy. On the weekends, she planned time outdoors to combine exercise with family time, taking her camera along as her love for photography was rekindled when she began using her phone camera as an exploration tool.

Hanna credits these brief touch points throughout the day for helping her remember what it was like to have an open heart. Her practice now is trying to live from that place as often as possible.

Like Hanna, you can experience wholehearted living through self-exploration wellness practices. In time you'll come to see that wellness does not merely involve physical or emotional change, it is a form of self-respect.

2

framework overview

When speaking with clients and colleagues, it's clear that there is little I can tell them about wellness that they don't already know. I bet you'd agree that it's better to eat healthier meals, move more, sleep deeply, minimize stress, and be kind to yourself and others. What, then, gets in the way of making healthy changes?

Perhaps you have been looking for a life hack or a silver-bullet solution that will get you on the right track. While there's no shortage of such advice, wellness shortcuts only provide a temporary boost or short-term relief.

Instead of quick fixes, let's take a look at what can get in the way of wellness success. Here are some common barriers to creating sustainable lifestyle change:

- **Perceived need for more resources** – Do you feel you need more money, time, gear or knowledge to create a healthier life? The desire to begin at an advanced level can sometimes derail beginning at all.

- **Unrealistic expectations** – Do your priorities align with your actions? A flat abs dream cannot be achieved with a sporadic, low-intensity workout regimen and no change in diet.

- **Slow or no progress** – Have you made some healthy changes but your progress has plateaued? Perhaps you are working against yourself in some way (e.g., feeling like you "should" be working out, comparing yourself to others, trying to outwork a poor diet).

- **Interest vs. commitment** – Do you have only casual interest in an activity? Sporadic activity will not produce the same results as a committed approach.

- **Not wanting to change** – Are you comfortable in your current lifestyle and hesitant to upset the status quo? As Tony Robbins once said, "Change happens when the pain of staying the same is greater than the pain of change."

As a wellness coach, I'm focused on driving behavioral change that increases engagement and productivity to help my clients live their best possible lives. This means helping them form a clear picture of the life they want to live and the challenges they're facing, and providing recommendations to help them build a workable action plan. It's my job to be an ally and cheerleader who helps them ensure all their hard work and progress are sustainable.

The Athena Principles methodology recognizes that wellness is a fluid process that thrives with a flexible approach. It regards wellness as a practice, honors and cultivates inner knowing, and provides accountability as well as the ability to celebrate wins or adjust as needed. The Principles can provide you with a foundation for making change, a vantage point to help you see where you're working against yourself, and a scalable process that can grow with you.

The Wellness Journey

In the previous chapter, we met Hanna, whose inner critic berated her for not taking better care of herself. Upon deeper reflection, she began to understand that the life she was living was not emulating what mattered most to her. That insight led her on a journey toward wholehearted living.

Hanna began with small steps. First, she began jotting her thoughts down in a small notebook she always had within reach. Then she began taking pictures with her phone of whatever moved her during the day.

She also started using the voice memo function on her phone to capture personal insights she had during the day. These small points of connection began to give her clues to areas of interest, like creating a map of new places to explore.

You can use *The Athena Principles* framework as the map for your journey toward increased vitality and well-being, which, in turn, can lead to living in a more wholehearted manner. We'll use the exercises in this chapter as tools to provide clarity and determine your destination. The Principles are the fuel that will get you from Point A to Point B and keep you on course. The practices will help you make the most of your experience by giving you perspective and creating a travelogue of your journey with the ability to look back and reflect at key turning points.

The Athena Principles Framework

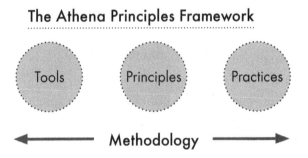

The Athena Principles is a framework comprised of a **methodology** that is a system of tools, Principles and practices that provide ways of teaching, learning and performing. It also includes:

- **Tools** to assess a current state of wellness, provide clarity, track progress, and set new objectives

- **Principles**, which are broad philosophical statements that provide a solid foundation and serve as a guide for current actions and future decisions

- **Practices** and activities that, when performed regularly, aim to create good habits and increased well-being.

Tools: The Holistic Wellness Spectrum

The Spectrum is a broad wellness inventory that can help you determine where to begin your wellness journey. It can be used repeatedly and is a useful tool to find new entry points to further increase wellness once progress has been made in other areas.

The Spectrum is categorized into three sections. The first is **Vitality** and it includes a list of familiar exercise and nutrition activities. Vitality is where most people start when they think about taking positive steps toward enhanced well-being.

The next section is **Flow** and it includes ideas for simplifying life routines, living intuitively and finding meaning and purpose.

The last section is **Connection**, and it includes a list of contemplative practices and ways of connecting in our relationships and community.

You will be using this Spectrum to determine your initial wellness focus area in a bit.

Holistic Wellness Spectrum

VITALITY		FLOW			CONNECTION	
Exercise & Nutrition		*Simplifying, Energetic Flow & Expression*			*Spirituality & Relationships*	
MOVE	NOURISH	SIMPLIFY	FLOW	CREATE	CONTEMPLATE	CONNECT
• Train	• Clean Nutrition	• Let Go	• Presence	• Expression	• Spirituality	• Intimate Relationship
• Aerobic	• Plant-based	• Possessions	• Intention	• Ideas	• Inner Work	• Family
• Strength	• Paleo/Keto/Zone	• People	• Discernment	• Visual Art	• Reflection	• Friends
• Functional	• Hybrid	• Ways of Being	• Deliberate Action	• Writing	• Lovingkindness	• Aligned Tribe
• Stretch/Roll	• Hydrate	• Empty Space	• Intuitive Living	• Music	• Compassion	• Holding Space/Depth
• Massage	• Supplement	• Mindful Consumption	• Own Rhythm	• Acting/Dance	• Generosity	• Empathy
• Recover	• Blended Meals	• Tech Detox	• Ease	• Explore	• Gratitude	• Support
• Sleep	• Intermittent Fasting	• Surroundings That Reflect Current Self	• Heartful	• Inspire	• Ritual	• Mentor
• Physical Health	• Wild/Local Food	• Morning/Evening Routines	• Positive Mindset	• Purpose	• Quest	• Social Circle
• Energy Management	• Healthy Recipes		• Financial Health	• Impact	• Nature	• Celebration
• Stress Management	• Food Preparation		• Volunteer	• Aligned Livelihood	• Listen	• Fun/Play
• Self-care	• Systems/Support			• Ongoing Learning	• Mediate	• Adventure
					• Rejuvinate	
					• Legacy	

Tools: The Wellness Assessment

Think back to the last time you were in a large setting, such as an airport or a shopping mall. Most likely there was an illustration depicting the layout of the environment and a red circle with the words "You are here."

The wellness assessment will provide a similar depiction of where you are in your journey and it can be completed in under five minutes. It's a simple evaluation used to rate where your current level of satisfaction is in each of the Holistic Wellness Spectrum categories.

Let's begin with examples of how I would have used the assessment at three very different points in my life.

As I mentioned in the Introduction, I was not in optimal physical shape in my mid-thirties. In fact, I was feeling the effects of aging for the first time. I was traveling for work often, not exercising, drinking alcohol on a regular basis, eating unhealthy vegetarian food and getting little sleep. As a result, I gained 25 pounds before finding and following the Body for Life method.

Back then, I would have entered this process through the vitality section of the Holistic Wellness Spectrum and focused on nutrition and exercise. Having identified my starting point, I would have worked through the Principles with those areas of focus in mind.

As you can see in the following chart, I was least satisfied with my level of exercise and nutrition, whereas I felt great about my connection with loved ones.

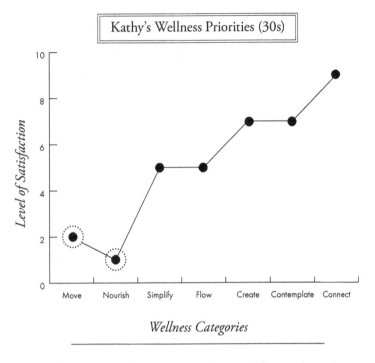

Kathy's Wellness Priorities (30s)

Level of Satisfaction

Wellness Categories

Fast forward a decade. My mid-forties brought a number of life changes and my wellness priorities adapted as a result. I began to get interested in different types of wellness activities (meditation, running) and eating styles (vegan, raw vegan). It was a decade of experimentation and I kept my weight mostly in check. Although I still did quite a bit of business travel, I continued to learn how to consistently move my body and make better nutritional choices, including drinking less alcohol.

It was a time of self-discovery and I spent a lot of energy reconnecting with my expressive self in the create section of the Holistic Wellness Spectrum through journaling and creative nonfiction writing.

I also began to explore quite a few elements in the contemplation pillar.

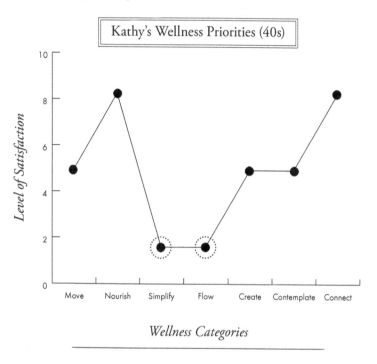

Kathy's Wellness Priorities (40s)

Wellness Categories

My sense of well-being really began humming as I entered my fifties. I learned how to put everything related to wellness that I had researched and experimented with together to create a cohesive – and comprehensive – approach that worked for me at midlife. I pushed myself to new physical limits, like relearning to ride a bike for the 275-mile Cycle for the Cause charity ride from Boston to New York City when I was 53, and completing my first marathon and ultra-marathon during an eight-week period when I was 54.

I learned to eat in alignment with my workout schedule and used natural remedies as ailments arose, such as adding fresh ginger to my diet to combat the inflammation from training. I also used complementary therapies that I credit with getting me across those event finish lines, such as foam rolling, acupuncture and massage.

Today, I have a solid nutrition and exercise program that's embedded into my daily routine. As my life shifted from a corporate-driven career to a creative and entrepreneurial one, my attention has been redirected to simplifying my life and learning how to make intentional choices to enhance flow. I'm also connecting with more people in a different way, developing deeper relationships in held space.

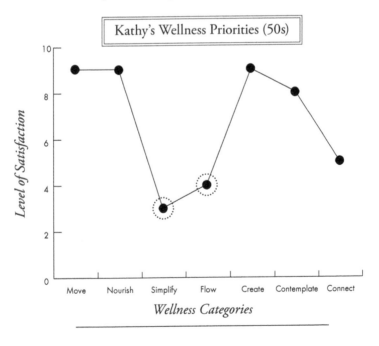

I put myself through this assessment process on an annual basis and revisit my progress throughout the year, reevaluating where I am at the six-month point. In addition, I check in with myself weekly to stay accountable and make any necessary changes to my approach.

As you can see from the series of assessments from my thirties through my fifties, wellness is dynamic. Everything on my Wellness Spectrum continues to evolve to this day and it feels empowering to be engaged in its continued development.

Why is this assessment so effective? Because it gives you an opportunity to step back and pinpoint activities that have been working well so they can be leveraged, as well as identify things that have been negatively impacting your wellness so they can be addressed. The Holistic Wellness Spectrum gives you a broad inventory to work with; it gives you a choice to start your wellness journey anywhere on the Spectrum – from exercise to connection – as well as add categories and activities that are critical to your personal well-being.

It also gives you a chance to reflect on why a particular starting point is best for you in this moment. For those under extreme work pressure, for example, a good place to start to increase wellness may be to decrease stress, not add to it. In this case, focusing on quality sleep or stress management will pay bigger dividends than adding the pressure of trying a new boot camp regimen.

Once a starting point has been identified, you can begin to make small but impactful changes.

Now it's your turn. Find a quiet spot where you know you'll be uninterrupted for a brief period of time. Close your eyes and take a few deep breaths to center yourself.

Scan the Holistic Wellness Spectrum. Without giving it too much logical thought, quickly run through each column and think about the level of happiness or satisfaction you feel as you review that area of wellness. Be open to any intuitive wisdom you may detect, even if it does not make sense in this moment.

Which areas have the greatest pull? Where to do you feel the most energy and heat? In what category would it be most beneficial right now to make incremental progress?

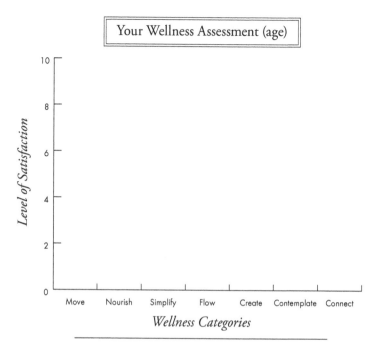

Your Wellness Assessment (age)

Level of Satisfaction

10

8

6

4

2

0

Move   Nourish   Simplify   Flow   Create   Contemplate   Connect

Wellness Categories

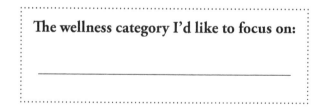

The wellness category I'd like to focus on:

_____

This simple exercise puts the power of change in your hands. You are the architect of your wellness journey and can customize the program to fit your own needs and lifestyle.

Principles: The Athena Principles

The word "principle" is defined as "a fundamental truth that serves as the foundation for a system, belief, behavior or a chain of reasoning."

For a wellness framework to be effective, it must be easily applied. We each have unique life situations and histories that inform our mindset, needs, and abilities to address our current challenges.

I see *The Athena Principles* as a means of focusing and guiding your efforts no matter the circumstances, like guardrails for your wellness journey. You'll reference the Principles repeatedly as you implement positive changes and experience growth.

Here is a brief overview of the Principles we'll be exploring in depth in the following chapters:

- **Principle 1 – Self-Compassion:** The care for one's own well-being in the form of self-acceptance and nurturing support.

- **Principle 2 – Intention:** Intentions help us aim, set direction and connect emotionally to what we want. It's the heart-based "Why" behind the urge to transform.

- **Principle 3 – Consistency:** This is the secret component to the whole equation. Consistency is how you choose to show up for yourself and stay committed and engaged throughout the process, especially during challenging times.

- **Principle 4 – Growth Mindset:** How you view the wellness journey will determine your progress and enjoyment. Applying a growth mindset where challenges are seen as opportunities will position you to move forward with grace and ease.

- **Principle 5 – Accountability:** A systematic way to check-in with what you commit to accomplish, celebrate the wins, and compassionately adjust where needed.

As we move through the Principles, you can use this Wellness Action Plan Worksheet for any notes relating to your wellness assessment and reflections on the process so far.

Wellness Action Plan Worksheet		
Area of focus:	Week of:	
Principle	**Key Points and Actions**	**Progress**
❶ Self-Compassion		
❷ Intention		
❸ Consistency		
❹ Growth Mindset		
❺ Accountability		
Observations from this week/adjustments for next:		

Downloadable versions of the tools included in this book are available at www.AthenaWellness.com.

Practices: Writing as a Wellness Practice

For many people, the thought of writing can stir fears akin to public speaking, towering heights, and colossal spiders. Before explaining the science of why writing is a good wellness practice, let me assure you – if you can write an email or send a text, you have the ability to write your way toward wellness. You won't be sharing your writing, unless you choose, and you are free to discard your work, although it's advisable to keep it.

"By establishing a writing practice, you are creating a safe place for learning what wholehearted living means for you."

If you enjoy writing or keeping a journal, these practices will fit right into your routine. If you don't enjoy narrative writing, no worries. You can use a bulleted list, your phone's notes, audio, video and camera capabilities, and if you are more artistic, you can use the writing practice as a time to doodle, sketch, paint or collage. If you want portable or virtual options, you can also use an online journal, some of which are multimedia.

By establishing a writing practice, you are creating a safe place for learning what wholehearted living means for you. Consider your writing practice as a protected space – a private sanctuary, if you will, in which you can:

- Identify where your outer and inner selves are not congruent
- Explore areas of interest that have been long ignored but where you still feel a spark

- Dive deep and have fearless conversations with yourself, mining for the hidden treasures in the depths of your soul.

Why is writing considered a wellness practice?

There have been numerous studies since the 1980s linking writing practice to a boost in immunity, cell revitalization, and ease from depression. The most cited researcher is Dr. James W. Pennebaker, a professor at the University of Texas at Austin, who has written several books on the topic.

Dr. Pennebaker is a proponent of expressive writing in which the writer connects with the underlying emotion of a chosen topic. He believes that writing is a powerful tool for healing. He has stated that holding back thoughts and feelings can place people at risk for various levels of disease. Over time, a regular writing practice can lead to less stress and better sleep.

For our purposes, we'll focus on using writing as a tool to enhance mindfulness by taking a few minutes each day to be present and demonstrate self-discipline by showing up for yourself on the page.

Think of your notebook as a place where you can:

- Listen when life speaks

- Express anything without explaining yourself

- Explore who you are

- Capture your creative sparks
- Begin to reclaim the neglected parts of yourself.

Your notebook is a place where you can express your heart unapologetically and feel free to dialogue with your Inner Wilderness, the untamed territory of your soul. Writing, in short, will allow you to align with new and emerging energy while developing language and tools to live from your wholehearted self.

Practices: Meditation as a Wellness Practice

Another contemplative exercise we'll explore is mindfulness meditation. Meditation is a centuries-old practice that helps center inward attention. It can be practiced in a number of ways including focusing on breath, sound, a repeated phrase or through physical movement.

The benefits of the practice include a positive impact to the nervous system, including lower blood pressure, cortisol, and anxiety levels, which result in less stress and enhanced wellness. As we get into the Principles we will practice mindful self-compassion techniques, which is the acceptance of the present moment while offering ourselves what is most needed for our well-being.

chapter 3

readying for the journey

I felt an enticing pull to attend my first writing retreat when I was 46 years old. Until that point I had been scribbling in notebooks for more than 20 years but had never shared my writing with anyone nor did I share my aspiration to be a writer beyond my partner and a few close friends.

For some inexplicable reason, however, I felt compelled to attend a week-long writing workshop on Whidbey Island, located an hour north of Seattle, Washington. This experience held the spark that completely transformed my life and began the third and deepest phase of my wellness journey.

It was as if the perfect storm of circumstances converged for my benefit, including venturing out of my comfort zone by:

- Traveling to and living in an unfamiliar place
- Sharing space with and learning from writers with different life experiences and ways of being
- Learning upon arrival that we'd be entering silence for 36 hours toward the end of the week.

During the silent portion of the retreat, I finally quieted enough to listen to my inner knowing, which proved to be so powerful, not only did I write an impactful piece, but I learned how to access that quiet wisdom for clarity ever since. In the hush, I also caught glimpses of the heart-based future life I desired, which was far from the left-brained place I was living at the time and almost exactly how I live today.

Those sagacious insights helped me step into my own power, and in doing so, I began to make wellness decisions that were more in line with what my future self would expect.

This rare combination of events was masterfully orchestrated by an experienced facilitator who helped guide me through this uncharted personal territory. The key takeaways that I incorporated into my life included the importance of:

- Listening in the quiet and stillness regularly
- Connecting with my deeper self through writing

- Learning to live from an open heart by working through the places where I wasn't being true to myself to move closer to my inner light and essence.

This may sound rudimentary, but huge life shifts happened in the wake of this experience to support the new vision I had for myself. It also gave me the opportunity to cultivate my new open-hearted learnings in "the real world" as a deep practice that continues today. It's a practice that is never ending and one that pays big dividends in optimizing my well-being at midlife. It's this practice that *The Athena Principles* was built upon.

"It has been my experience that when I'm aligned with my truest self, I take better care of myself. As a result, my experience of life is calm, joyful and filled with meaning."

It has been a decade since my life-changing experience on Whidbey Island and since that time I have applied the Principles to different areas of the Holistic Wellness Spectrum repeatedly. It has been my experience that when I'm aligned with my truest self, I take better care of myself. As a result, my experience of life is calm, joyful and filled with meaning.

This doesn't mean that life is without tension, which can be especially prominent when moving from old life patterns to new ones. I have found, however, that when I'm connected to what matters most to me, I am able to better navigate the sometimes rough waters of life's challenges and better appreciate the beauty of my journey.

I wrote *The Athena Principles* to provide an easy and repeatable method to help you move toward what matters most to you while taking good care of yourself along the way. But you will also need to rely on your own insight to keep you on the path that's right for you.

Guideposts, or signposts, provide directions for travelers, especially when paused at a crossroad, or critical decision point. Your notebook is the best place I know to connect with your inner wisdom to keep you on course.

If you haven't done so already, you'll need to have an easily accessible safe place to record your insights. Regardless of your method, whether you physically write them down or record them electronically, I will be referring to this place as your notebook for the remainder of the book.

The only rule is that your entries will need to be dated. You may also want to include the time of day and physical location, as I do.

Once you have your notebook, you'll be breaking it in by completing the three exercises at the end of this chapter.

How do you get ready for your own wellness journey? I'm aware of the rarity of having a week to yourself like I did. Such a luxury is not required to practice the Principles. Instead, you will be able to set your own timeframe and work pace.

So far during our time together, you have acquired your map (the Principles and methodology) and your preliminary destination (area of focus from your wellness assessment). There are a few additional points to consider that may further support you during the journey ahead.

Flexibility

Any seasoned traveler knows the importance of having a Plan B and enough flexibility to use it because even meticulous trip planning can go awry. This doesn't give us an excuse not to execute our plans, but it does give us upfront permission to listen deeply and make adjustments according to our own inner knowing.

For example, you may have decided on exercise as an area of focus when you completed your wellness assessment in the last chapter. Your primary destination, then, will be to incorporate more movement into your life.

As you begin to work through the Principles and create a little quiet time to complete the writing practices, you may be surprised by what your self-awareness reveals. You may feel energized by the thought of creatively expressing yourself, or you may feel the need to get more sleep, or you may expand your meditation time from five minutes each day to fifteen.

It's okay to take the scenic route and explore what it might feel like to incorporate some of these things into your life, either in addition to (exercise and meditation), in place of (meditation instead of exercise), or combined with your original destination (a meditative running practice).

You may find that you choose to stick with your original plan, which is great, but be willing to explore and adjust the course along the way. Just know it's okay to go "off road," see the sights, and take the long way.

Expectations

If you were planning a vacation, you would want to make sure you have enough resources to meet your desired experience. For your wellness journey, your budget currency is time, but it, too, should be linked to your desired outcome.

Does the time you're looking to devote to enhanced well-being align with your outcome expectations? If your goal is simply to add more movement to your week, a 15-minute walk at lunchtime Monday through Friday might be enough. If you're looking to train for a triathlon, the time commitment and intensity will need to be aligned accordingly.

If you are just starting down the wellness path or getting back into a routine after time away, devoting less time and celebrating small wins are appropriate, as these little victories will accumulate over time and before long, you'll see big progress.

The following exercises are designed to help prepare you to work through the Principles and related practices:

1. **Addition/Subtraction:** To keep a list of who or what boosts and depletes your energy

2. **Role Deconstruction:** To mine current roles for hidden costs and hidden values

3. **A Perfect Day:** To begin to practice listening to your inner-knowing.

EXERCISE #1

Addition and Subtraction

This exercise was designed as an easy way to begin to get in touch with how you're feeling. We'll use the output in a future chapter.

- In your notebook, write two headings: "What Lights Me Up" and "What Depletes My Energy."

- Begin to list the people, places, things, experiences, roles, and responsibilities that add to your life force or detract from it.

- Add items to the list whenever you feel moved to do so.

+	**-**
Lights Me Up!	Depletes My Energy
1.	1.
2.	2.
3.	3.
. . .	. . .
100.	100.

EXERCISE #2

Role Deconstruction

This exercise is especially helpful for Type A personalities (yes, my hand is raised!). It will help clarify the roles you're currently playing and how you'd like to leverage and nurture your current traits for future use. It will also begin to show gaps in areas where you may want to learn new skills or old behaviors that you'd like to drop.

- Examine your "superwoman/man" identity by breaking it into five main components or roles. For example: partner, mom, executive, caregiver for aging parents, and runner.

- Further explore each one as follows:

   - **Function:** What purpose does this role serve in your life? For example, as an executive, you may enjoy a steady paycheck but be challenged by scheduled work times and related business travel. You can weigh the pros and cons to adjust accordingly. You may also look for opportunities to make the most of this role, perhaps by going back to school or getting a certification in an area that's of interest to you.

- **Traits:** What types of personality traits do you embody in that role? What's your brand? As an executive, you may be dependable, reliable, always prepared, etc.

- **Behaviors:** How do you operate at your best and worst in each role? As an executive, you may be the meticulous professional at best and stressed and exhausted at worst.

- **Nourish:** How might you best care for yourself when playing this role? To alleviate the feeling of being trapped in an office, perhaps you can schedule a lunchtime walk whenever possible to reconnect with yourself.

- **Integrate:** How might you begin to integrate this role with your deeper self or consider changing it if it doesn't align? You can try to make your workday more palatable by learning something new, reading, or researching topics of interest.

As you go through the exercise at this stage, focus on the first three categories. We'll be working through strategies to nourish and integrate your roles as we learn more about the Principles and complete the exercises.

For now, you can keep notes on the roles you want to change, drop or expand.

	Function	Traits	Behaviors	Nourish	Integrate
(Partner)					
(Mom)					
(Executive)					
(Caregiver)					
(Runner)					

EXERCISE #3

A Perfect Day

One of the things that stops many people from living an intention-based life is that getting started can seem like a big task. Experts on the topic commonly suggest starting with questions like: What matters most to you? What's your purpose? Or what makes you feel happy? These simple questions can seem overwhelming and impossible to answer while you're in the middle of actioning a broad range of responsibilities in your current life.

I struggled with similar questions when I was contemplating leaving corporate life and becoming an entrepreneur. At that time, I was fortunate to work with Amanda Cook, who is both a digital marketing and health coach with a focus on wellness entrepreneurs, or wellpreneurs. Overwhelmed by the big "life purpose" question, Amanda guided me through an exercise from her book, Wellpreneur. She had me envision how I wanted to feel at work and in life once my wellness business was up and running.

I've adapted the exercise for our purposes. You may wish to record the questions on your phone. Take a few deep breaths and be open to whatever images and feelings surface.

Close your eyes and imagine a future day in your life when you are feeling great about all the areas on the Holistic Wellness Spectrum of Vitality, Flow and Connection. You also may choose to focus on the area you highlighted in the exercise you completed in the previous chapter.

- See yourself waking up.

- Where are you? Where do you live? Who is with you?

- What's your morning routine like? What do you have for breakfast? Do you exercise?

- How do you spend your day? Are you working? Where? Doing what? If not, what did you do with your time?

- What do you eat during the day?

- What are your home surroundings like? How does the space feel?

- What do you do for fun? Do you create anything? Learn anything new?

- Do you spend any time in contemplation? Out in nature?

- Who do you spend time with? How does it feel to be with them? How does it feel to connect with your loved ones?

- What do you do at night? What is your evening routine like?

- What are you most enthusiastic about in your life? What's on the horizon in the months and years ahead that has you excited and motivated?

- How do you feel about your life and work?

- What are you looking forward to in the future?

- Does anything else surface for you?

Once you're done, spend ten minutes free-writing in your notebook. What comes to mind as you reflect on the questions? The specific details are not as important as the feelings you capture on the page. This will be insightful for setting wellness intentions that align with your true desires, which you'll learn about in Chapter Five.

There will be more opportunities for hands-on activities in the next five chapters that outline each Principle. At the end of those chapters is a section that includes a writing exercise, a meditation, and an experiential activity related to the Principle.

Let's take a moment to pause and appreciate all the ground you've covered so far – such as identifying an area of wellness focus, starting your writing practice, and envisioning your perfect day. Now you're well prepared for the journey ahead, which will start with Principle 1 – Self-Compassion, learning to better understand, accept and love ourselves.

chapter

4

principle #1:

self-compassion

The care for one's own well-being
in the form of self-acceptance and nurturing support.

The benefits of self-compassion are broad. Research has shown it can improve self-worth, motivation, depression, body image and overall happiness. People who have self-compassion practices develop the ability to administer kindness to themselves as soon as they recognize they are hurting.

Our threat responses become elevated when we're under stress, which can be compounded by self-critical thoughts. Chronic stress keeps this response heightened. This can impact the major systems in our body:

- **Respiratory** – shallow or erratic breathing
- **Cardiovascular** – rapid pulse and increased blood pressure raising the risk of heart attacks or strokes
- **Endocrine** – production of hormones such as adrenaline and cortisol, a hormone that can lead to increased appetite and the accumulation of fat tissue stored around the midsection
- **Gastrointestinal** – nerves in the intestinal tract can be triggered resulting in digestive problems like nausea, inflammation and spasm
- **Musculoskeletal** – increased muscle tension leading to chronic pain or migraines
- **Immune** – lowered response to disease and infection.

While research has established the correlation between self-compassion and higher levels of wellness, recent studies indicate that showing yourself kindness and acceptance can actually switch off your threat responses.

This doesn't mean that the perceived threats, such as the fear of losing a job, disappear. It means that the people who have routine self-compassion practices are better equipped to handle the circumstance. It's the difference between emotionally reacting to a situation and calmly responding to it.

Self-care practices are like deposits in the bank – they are reserve resources you can build and drawn upon when needed.

As a coach, it's my job to understand that when clients come to me with a specific change they'd like to make, their desired shift is usually bigger than what they are directly stating. One of the keys of good coaching is to create a space for clients where they feel comfortable and safe enough to explore places in their psyche that have long been hidden or are possibly unknown.

How do you create a safe space for yourself without a coach? As noted in the previous chapter, your notebook is that space. It can be used to dialogue with yourself, as a way to feel heard, and as a step toward reclaiming your true self. Use it as a place to question, where there's no need to explain yourself. Use it as a place to listen and know you're okay no matter what comes up.

In addition to writing in your notebook, I'd also recommend you begin to find a time where you can be kind and gentle with yourself, where your only purpose is to relax into a tender place of discovery and non-judgment.

You can be creative with how you choose to connect with yourself and find time to be with your thoughts:

- Ten minutes before you get out of bed to start the day
- In your car during your commute to work
- On an extended walk to a meeting around the perimeter of your office building
- During a midday or after-dinner stroll
- During a weekly scheduled meeting with yourself at a local coffee shop to write in your notebook
- Giving yourself ten minutes to experience a mindful pause in a comfy chair
- On an evening walk with the dog
- While stepping outside to look at the night sky
- On a long bike ride, run or hike
- During the five minutes before you close your eyes at the end of the day.

Be consistent in claiming your space, even if it's just five or ten minutes at a time. As you routinely settle into a quiet space for yourself, you'll find you want to spend more time there.

You will also begin to feel the value of meeting yourself where you are and having a place to explore your self-doubt and fears as well as your desires. In the process, you also may identify wellness strategies you've tried that have not produced the desired results and feel motivated to develop alternative ones.

Holding space for yourself means being fully present and providing unconditional support for your needs. It's a space you'll crave as you begin to trust your inner wisdom and move toward increased well-being.

Changing Inner Criticism to Inner Wisdom

Maria is a 49-year-old partner at a management consulting firm, the kind of person who appears to have it all together with a starched and pressed appearance that exudes confidence. She recently earned a big promotion as a global director responsible for hundreds of employees. The thrill of the promotion was short-lived, however.

Since the beginning of her career, Maria has taken good care of herself, working out in the mornings and keeping an eye on her sugar and caffeine consumption. However, when she started her new position, Maria's work commitments began to take more time, infringing on her early workouts. As a result, she began to crave a boost in the afternoon reaching for something sweet, a cup of coffee, or both. Within months she started to notice weight gain.

Maria also began experiencing bouts of insomnia for the first time in her life. She would wake around midnight with a start, her heart racing and skin glistening with sweat. The more she worried about experiencing another sleepless night, the higher her anxiety level rose.

It didn't help that she filled the endless nighttime hours by replaying various scenes from her workday, criticizing herself whenever she perceived she had failed to meet her own high standards. Knowing her clients loved working with her and that the firm promoted her because she consistently delivered an excellent product put even more pressure on her to perform.

In the middle of the night, Maria's fears surfaced. She felt like an imposter. She suffered from crippling doubt. She feared she wouldn't be able to continue to deliver, or worse, that her colleagues would realize she didn't deserve her new position. Ultimately, she feared losing her job altogether because she would not be able to meet the firm's expectations over the long run. She also worried that the lack of sleep and reduced activity would negatively impact the wellness protocols that had worked so well for her in the past.

The inner critic is that internal voice that provides commentary on our actions throughout the day. Its voice is fear-based, its tone is critical and judgmental, and it can impact our self-esteem. It can surface at inopportune moments, such as when considering a change or trying something new, listing all the reasons why continuing with the status quo is the safer bet.

The inner voice is developed during childhood as we learn right from wrong from our primary caregivers – that is, what behaviors are expected and rewarded and vice versa. It's the voice that tells us what we "should" do and how we "should" behave in line with the expectations of society and those with authority.

The difficulty arises when the inner voice remains at the developmental level, perhaps mimicking a parent, teacher or authority figure from decades past. While its original job was to help us learn to behave when we were children, the inner voice can negatively impact our sense of identity as we get older, especially when it speaks in a disapproving tone, compares us to others, and dutifully notes where we're falling short.

"When we remove emotion from the equation and begin to deconstruct the inner voice, we usually find this bully of a presence may, in fact, be terrified – of taking risks, of failing, and of getting hurt."

When we pay attention to our inner talk track as adults, it's often sobering to hear the tone and words we use with ourselves. For example, we may hear the inner voice when we wake and are thinking about going to the gym. The inner dialogue may start with how comfortable it is in bed and how nice another hour of sleep would be instead of getting up and working out.

It can get progressively worse from there. You may hear your inner voice saying, *What's one more day of not working out*, *You're too old for this*, and *You're out of shape*, among a litany of other comments meant to keep you safe from new or vulnerable situations.

When we believe the inner critic, we find ourselves operating in a state of emotional reactivity, which can lead to feelings of isolation or the need to strive for perfection, among other behaviors that can result in a reduced quality of life and even depression. That spiral can continue to impact our wellness in the form of unhealthy habits, such as inactivity or numbing ourselves with food, alcohol or social media dopamine hits.

Recognizing and learning to work with the inner critic is key to developing self-compassion because it's not just the words you hear from the inner talk track, it's the related feelings it can generate, such as inadequacy, shame or guilt.

When we remove emotion from the equation and begin to deconstruct the inner voice, we usually find this bully of a presence may, in fact, be terrified – of taking risks, of failing, and of getting hurt. Like the man behind the curtain in the Wizard of Oz, you may find this critical inner voice is really meant to keep you safe from experiences that remind you of those that caused you pain in the past.

Those unpleasant past experiences, along with the lessons we learned growing up that helped us discern right from wrong, comprise what psychologist Carl Jung called the personal shadow, or the disowned self. This shadow self is made up of all the parts of us that we hide or don't want to acknowledge out of a need to belong.

From Jung's perspective, there is no wholeness without both the light and the shadow of ourselves, and the more we embrace our imperfections, the healthier we become because the shadow loses its power under the light of examination.

Poet Robert Bly characterized the shadow self more eloquently with an image of a child putting all the unwanted parts of his shadow in an invisible bag and dragging it behind him throughout his life.

A critical part of self-compassion is fully accepting ourselves, including our light and dark aspects. The benefits of exploring the shadow self include:

- **Enhanced wellness** in the form of increased energy from releasing the invisible psychological weight. This energetic boost is caused by no longer needing to pull, suppress or protect what was being carried in secret.

- **Increased authenticity** as your self-understanding allows you to see yourself and others with more clarity and empathy.

- **Deeper relationships with yourself and others** as you accept and own more of your story, become more confident in the day-to-day, and feel less triggered by emotions or external events.

How do you begin to listen to and work with your inner voice and shadow self? First, by becoming aware of when the talk track starts and pausing to analyze the messages you're sending yourself.

Using the gym example, ask yourself: "Is there any truth to what I'm hearing about the benefit of sleeping through my workout and that I'm too out of shape to exercise in some way?" As you listen to the voice inside, can you identify where the commentary is exaggerated or blown out of proportion? Can you relate it to an uncomfortable feeling from a past experience?

Once you've listened to and acknowledged the message, note how it makes you feel. How will you feel later in the day when you're at work and you didn't go to the gym? Will you be disappointed in yourself? Conversely, how will you feel if you go, even if you don't work out at full capacity? Will you feel proud of yourself and motivated to try harder next time?

Try to explore what the inner voice is protecting you from. Did you feel embarrassed or awkward the last time you went to the gym? Can you thank the inner critic for bringing it to your attention and find another way, perhaps walking in your neighborhood instead of going to a health club?

If you find yourself in an endless loop of critical internal replay, perhaps you can change your environment by engaging in an activity that shifts your thoughts. You can go back and analyze the situation for any grains of truth once the related emotion passes.

When you find a particularly nagging theme coming from your critical inner voice (e.g., "Don't exercise today, you'll embarrass yourself."), analyze it in your notebook. Write out the critical view and then counter it with a fact-based rational view. For example:

Inner voice (IV): "Don't get up and go the gym, you need sleep more than exercise."

Inner wisdom (IW): "I promised myself I would work out four times this week. It's Monday and I want to get a good start."

IV: "But you felt so out of place the last time you went. You have old workout clothes that don't fit you right and you're at least 20 years older than everyone there. You don't even recognize the music they play and the volume - it's so loud!"

IW: "Maybe so, but I know how I'll feel later in the day if I don't go. I'll be disappointed in myself and I don't like that feeling. I'd rather hear loud pop music I don't like at 6 a.m."

IV: "It's only Monday. Sleep in today and go tomorrow."

IW: "I'm going this morning and will make a note to get some new workout clothes I'm comfortable in. This will get easier."

As you continue the dialogue, what you will most likely discover is that ongoing analysis will help you get to the root of the feeling and perhaps to a related action and/or a key learning.

Learning is an opportunity. In my corporate life, I used the situations where I didn't feel on par with my peers to upgrade my skills. For example, after giving my first presentation as a new manager early in my career, I knew I could do better. I didn't feel that my talk track flowed and I felt very nervous throughout. My boss suggested that I volunteer to teach for the professional organization that governed the work we did. This entailed getting a professional certification and then going through a selection and training process. Once I became a trainer, I taught for that organization for ten years. It paid dividends and was the main reason I was comfortable presenting to the Board of Directors for Fortune 250 companies later in my career.

That same skill proved invaluable when my inner voice rose up as I contemplated leaving the corporate world to become an entrepreneur. At first it seemed I would be starting from scratch, leaving all that I knew behind as I began to turn my passion for wellness into a viable business. But in dialoguing in my notebook with what my inner voice was trying to tell me, I learned that not only was I holding onto old beliefs, such as there's only one way to make a living, but I also realized all the skills I had accumulated over the decades were applicable to my new venture.

That's the real turning point – when you can shift the voice of the inner critic to the voice of a supportive ally. This takes practice and does not happen overnight. It can begin through dialoguing with the inner voice as I did. Even simpler, you can start by adding your favorite term of endearment after a harsh critique by your inner critic. For example, if you catch yourself saying, "This is never going to work," change it to "This is never going to work, love." It will feel a little strange, and that's the point. It pushes the inner critic out of its comfort zone. In time, the dialogue will shift to something more helpful, such as "How can we get this to work, *love*? How about we…"

That's when your inner criticism begins to turn into inner wisdom.

An Invitation to Tea

The key to befriending your shadow self is the acceptance of what it has to offer. The willingness to discover the repressed, disowned or unlived parts of your life, along with curiosity to delve into what's hidden in your shadow, is like an invitation to explore your Inner Wilderness.

How do you begin to do this work? Perhaps you enjoyed a certain activity when you were younger that you pushed away in order to fully embrace your adult responsibilities. Perhaps you kept a creative hobby secret or buried the impulse to be more spiritual. These suppressed pursuits can be fertile ground to explore why a part of your former self was reprioritized. In your notebook you can explore the impact it's having on your life today. You can also experiment with ways to bring these hidden parts forward in your everyday life by engaging in a related activity or learning about a new topic that seems to be tugging at you, taking small steps to integrate what was kept veiled.

There is a story from the Buddha's life on how he handled his shadow side, embodied by an otherworldly entity called Mara. Whenever Mara, who represented the Buddha's ego, would attack with thoughts ranging from fear to doubt to craving, the Buddha would not run, fight or push Mara away. Instead, every time the shadow would beckon, the Buddha would react the same way. He would recognize the presence of the shadow and say, "I see you, Mara. Let's have some tea."

Recognizing the presence of what you'd rather reject and befriending it doesn't make it go away. Rather, it becomes a practice of being with what is without judgment, which is a way to deal with what's at hand mindfully and move on with non-reaction. It also reinforces that you are showing up for yourself with compassion, much like you would a dear friend in need.

A helpful practice in difficult moments is one of self-inquiry: What am I feeling? What do I need in this moment? Naming what is happening, acknowledging that it's hard and giving yourself credit for your efforts is a powerful way to accept and shift emotion.

The Still Point of Self-Compassion Practice

Allowing room for all your emotions without judgment ultimately brings you to a still point – the spacious calm where you are detached from thoughts and in a peaceful place of surrender and release, like a wave rising, falling and returning to the ocean.

Self-compassion practices can act as still points in your day, as a place to get quiet and listen to yourself. These practices can be a break from the daily activity, noise and intensity of modern life.

In quiet moments, we can more easily identify causes of tension and stress, which, as noted earlier in this chapter, can negatively impact our major body functions. Mindful pauses allow us to listen for what's important and what's needed to best care for ourselves. In other words, we can connect with how to make the best choice for ourselves in that moment.

Self-compassion practices can be quite simple and for our purposes they are grouped into four categories:

- **Mindfulness:** The practice of being aware of your mind, body, and feelings in the present moment.

- **Lovingkindness:** The practice of sending goodwill toward yourself and others.

- **Self-forgiveness:** The process of letting go of negative feelings around a situation by no longer punishing yourself for your own mistakes nor blaming those who have wronged you. The freedom is in the release.

- **Gratitude:** Reflection of and appreciation for the people and experiences for which one is thankful. It's the feeling of being blessed.

In your notebook, jot down these four headings and describe any initial reactions you have when reading through them. Where do you feel the most resistance to these practices? Which practice do you think you'd like to explore?

During her sleepless nights, Maria began using her awake hours to explore her inner critical voice and why she silently spoke to herself in such a negative manner. What she realized was that the self-discipline that set her apart from her peers at work was fueled by a driving taskmaster within. While her inner voice could be hard on her, it had also helped her achieve all her accomplishments, both personal and professional, up to that point in her life. She wondered if there was a way to be just as productive while being kinder to herself.

Maria also realized that the fear of failure was at the root of her middle of the night anxiety, as she never wanted to disappoint herself or others. She began to use her awake time to run through three scenarios related to her work life. First, she would visualize the worst-case – that she could not function at the level expected for her new position and she was fired. Then, she would envision what she could do to prevent the worst-case scenario. Lastly, she came up with a strategy for when her work plans veered a bit off course, such as when a meeting didn't go well or when she missed an interim deadline.

This didn't get Maria back to sleep any sooner, but it did stop the endless loops of "what ifs" and "should haves." As the weeks passed, Maria found herself sleeping better and when she did wake in the middle of the night, she didn't dread it as much.

In addition, Maria shifted and reprioritized her self-care practices. She used her weekends to get out for two hikes or runs so she only had to find two workdays during the week to go to the gym and tried to get one workout under her belt early in the week. She also set aside the first five or ten minutes of her morning commute to check in with herself.

Maria learned a lot during these brief touch points, and she began engaging her inner critic almost like a mentor. For example, when she was wrestling with a problem at work, she asked herself what kind of advice she would give a colleague who came to her for counsel with a similar problem. This simple technique usually helped her objectively frame the issue at hand by taking herself out of the picture.

Maria's sleepless nights still occur when she is stressed, but she now has the tools to work through them. She finds that the time spent in nature on the weekends is key for her, and as a result, she's more at ease at work and has a greater capacity to enjoy her personal time at home.

principle #1:
self-compassion

Writing Practice
....
Dialoguing with Your Shadow Self/Inner Wilderness

A simple way to get acquainted with your shadow self is through free writing, which is a technique used to bypass the inner critic and get to the underlying feelings.

The only rule in free writing is to keep your hand moving. There's no need to worry about punctuation, spelling, content or neatness. Just keep going. If you have nothing to say you can write, "I have nothing to say," or "This is dumb," or "Blah, blah, blah." Eventually, you'll get out of your own way and write what's really on your mind and in your heart.

Try this:

- Take out your notebook and write "I am…" at the top.

- Set the timer on your phone for 10 minutes.

- Begin with the words "I am" and complete the sentence based on how you're feeling and what's on your mind. For example, "I am not good enough, I am judgmental, I am the person who cut someone off on the highway going to work this morning, I am a distracted mother when I travel," etc.

- Whenever you complete a thought, write "I am" and begin again. Keep going until the timer sounds.

- Alternative writing prompts: If you really knew me..., People don't often see..., What if you knew...

The "I am" and alternative writing prompt exercises are a great first step to get to know your shadow self. We can feel shame for some of our darker "I ams," but naming our shadow qualities helps us take ownership of who we are and helps us incorporate our shadow instead of dragging it behind us as baggage.

You may also find that with repeated practice, you come to your Inner Wilderness. This is the untamed, unexpressed, unexplored territory of your soul – your creative side also known as the Golden Shadow. For example, in addition to the negative self-talk you may also find yourself writing: "I am creative, I am interested in art, I am open to traveling, I am curious about yoga," etc. Look for new interests and unexpected sparks! Then begin a dialogue with your Golden Shadow to find out how to best nourish, support and listen to her.

Meditation Practice
Mindful Self-Compassion

Mindful Self-Compassion is having the awareness to treat yourself as you would a friend in need. This sounds easier than it is in real life. The following four practices will help get you started.

1. Try this - Mindfulness:
This is a practice I used to do for five minutes after the alarm sounded each weekday morning during my corporate career. It's a wonderful way to make a little space and mindfully relax for a short time.

- Set your timer for five or more minutes.

- Place you right hand over your heart and close your eyes. Take a few deep breaths to relax.

- Quietly remind yourself there is nothing for you to do in this moment. There is no one to tend to and no decisions to make. Just be and enjoy the quiet of the present moment. Let go of regrets, thoughts of past actions or future plans. Know that you are okay and should your mind drift (it will), gently bring it back to the present moment.

After practicing this meditation and feeling spaciousness for a period of time, feel free to experiment. You may ask yourself what you are feeling or what you need in the present moment. Explore those questions in your notebook.

2. Try this – Lovingkindness (Metta):

This is a practice used to send benevolent sentiments to yourself and others.

- Set your timer, place your hand over your heart, if desired, and take a few deep breaths.

- Quietly repeat and reflect on the following phrases:

  - May I be happy

  - May I be peaceful

  - May I be healthy

  - May I be at ease

- Alternative #1: You may expand the phrases to include loved ones (May you be happy…) as well as someone you may be having difficulty with or further expand to the broader world (May all beings be happy…).

- Alternative #2: Change the phrases to wording that resonates with your specific situation (May I be safe, May I show myself kindness, May I accept myself as I am, etc.).

3. Try this – Self-forgiveness:

This is a practice of acknowledging your humanness in making mistakes.

- Bring to mind an incident that calls for self-forgiveness.

- In your notebook free write as real and raw as you can to let the emotions all out.

- Try to understand why you acted the way you did.

- Find the learning in the situation and the opportunity to grow from it.

- See the situation rise toward the sky, as if releasing a helium balloon.

- Send loving light to yourself, picturing yourself happy and free from carrying this burden.

4. *Try this – Gratitude:*

Among the many benefits of having a gratitude practice are increased health, optimism, and better relationships with yourself and others.

- Focus on a specific person, thing or event you encountered during the day that you appreciate. It can be as simple as the smile the person gave you as you were exiting the subway or the extra loaf of bread your neighbor dropped off that he baked earlier in the day.

- Keep a section in your notebook to jot down these moments.

- You can also do this exercise while walking, noting all the things you see that bring beauty into your life.

- You may also choose to involve family and friends by writing these moments on slips of paper and keeping them in a jar that's in a prominent location. Pick a time to read them out loud together, such as holiday like New Year's Day.

Positive Action Practice

Addition and Subtraction Exercise Follow-up

Refer back to the Addition and Subtraction exercise you did in Chapter Three.

- Review and reflect on the reasons behind the items on the "Lights Me Up/Depletes My Energy" list.
- Pick one "Lights Me Up" item and schedule a related activity this week.
- Pick one "Depletes My Energy" item and determine a way to minimize its impact this week.

principle #1:
self-compassion

- It's important to hold space for yourself.

- There's a link between self-compassion and well-being.

- Inner Criticism can be transformed into Inner Wisdom.

- Welcoming the shadow moves you toward self-acceptance and wholeness.

- The still point can be accessed through mindful self-compassion practices.

- In your carry-on:

  - Dialoguing with your Shadow Self and Inner Wilderness

  - Mindful self-compassion practices:

    - Mindfulness

    - Lovingkindness (Metta)

    - Self-forgiveness

    - Gratitude

  - Awareness and action related to what "Lights Me Up" and "Depletes My Energy"

chapter 5

principle #2:
intention

Intentions help us aim, set direction and connect emotionally to what we want – it's the heart-based "Why" behind the urge to transform.

Goals, resolutions, pledges, promises, vows – I've made them, and I'm guessing you have, too. We plan to eat better, move more, learn Italian, save money, start the business, travel internationally, clear out the clutter, write the book, learn to meditate, and volunteer more often, among many other tasks, in order to lead what we believe will be a better life. At the moment we declare a new way forward, we typically feel a great amount of enthusiasm and momentum. As we begin to take action, however, it's not unusual for that exhilaration to wane.

It's estimated that less than 10 percent of New Year's resolutions are achieved. The main reason for the low success rate is unrealistic outcome expectations, such as the speed and ease of achievement, that are not aligned with sustained effort. Self-help author Debbie Ford once wisely noted, "All of our suffering in life is from saying we want one thing and doing another."

Through the years I have traveled quite a bit for professional and personal reasons, meeting a lot of people along the way. It's not unusual for casual conversations to turn to wellness once people learn that I'm a coach. Someone I met five minutes prior will begin confiding how they feel the need to lose weight, eat better, exercise more – shameful confessions of all the things they feel they should be doing.

I listen until they are done with their admission and then ask them, "*Why* do you want to do those things?" That question is usually met with a brief moment of silence and a puzzled look, followed by a general response about wanting to feel better. Again, I'll ask with curiosity, "*Why?*"

What I'm gently trying to explore with my new acquaintances are their intentions beyond the goal-driven comparisons to others or expectations of society. I seek to find out what's really motivating them deep down.

What's the difference between a goal, and all of its synonyms, and an intention?

A goal is defined as "the end toward which effort is directed." Goals are future-oriented and focused on achievement. They reflect how we want to show up at a later date in our outer world.

An intention is defined as "a determination or resolve to act in a certain way." Intentions are rooted in the present and focused on living in alignment with beliefs and values. They reflect how we feel in our inner world.

More specifically:

Goals are	Intentions are

• Future-oriented
• Focused on external achievement
• Accomplish an end result
• Of the head
• Reflect our outer world persona
  - Plans
  - Abilities
  - Behaviors
  - Performance
  - Actions taken
  - Focused on "what's missing"
  - Depletes energy
  - Missed goals = failure
  - Achieved goals = success
	• Rooted in the present
	• Focused on alignment with beliefs and values
	• Embodied and lived each day
	• Of the heart
	• Reflect our inner world selves
	  - Includes feelings and desires
	  - Welcomes discovery
	  - Encourages non-judgement
	  - Acts as guidance for choices
	  - Connects to who we are
	  - Focuses on "what's possible"
	  - Increases energy
	  - Provides purpose
	  - Gives directional clarity

The reason why most New Year's resolutions fail is that they are usually goal-driven, with a focus on results and external rewards. Often, resolutions are not aligned with a strong internal desire, but instead with a sense of what should be done or wanted. The mindset of "succeed or fail" further adds stress to an already taxing behavioral change – which ultimately leads to failure.

Intentions are more forgiving. They honor the effort expended and the process embarked upon. They are designed for long-term change, as they are connected to the authentic self and, most importantly, contain the "Why" behind the desired change. And since they connect with our sense of worthiness, intentions lend themselves to self-compassionate action.

When a person looks to make a change, it's often because the change is something:

- They feel they *should* do (sign up for yoga, go to the gym, meditate)
- That's not good for them (obsessively checking their phone/social media, smoking, excessive drinking, emotional eating)
- They are avoiding (clearing clutter, doctor's visit, difficult discussion with their partner).

Of course, these are all very good reasons to implement change, but real change takes time. Some popular, oft-quoted research indicates it takes 21 days for a habit to shift, although recent findings show it takes closer to 66 days for a change to take hold. Two plus months is a long time to stay motivated without a driving force. Your "Why" keeps you going when you're feeling depleted, frustrated or tired.

Your "Why" allows you to identify what's at stake for you personally if you don't make the change. Your "Why" is your deep motivation – your call to action. It clarifies how you want to show up in the world. Once you know your "Why," the path forward (what, how, when, where, with whom) becomes more apparent.

Here's the process for setting an intention:

- Quietly check-in with yourself and see what change you'd like to cultivate. Look at your strengths, values, passions, and things that bring you joy. You can flip back to Chapter Two to remind yourself of the area of focus – i.e., nutrition, movement, meditation, sleep, etc. – you selected when you reviewed the Holistic Wellness Spectrum. (I've included my process from my 54th birthday intention setting session in parenthesis throughout this example.)

- If you're unsure where to start, consider what matters most to you. (I'm grateful for my health at midlife and want to learn more about the impact of exercise and nutrition on aging.)

  - What do you like to learn about?
  - What do you like to create?

- Is there something to start or stop doing?
- When do you feel in flow?
- Where does your heart feel full and aligned?
- What do you like to nurture?
- What nourishes you?
- What do you like to build?
- For whom and for what do you feel gratitude?

- Select an impactful change for you that resonates deeply and is important to make now. Be positive and keep the statement in the present tense. (I'm interested in learning how to challenge my body as I age and also treat it with care.)

- Make sure it's something you want to do rather than appease other people's expectations. (I can feel changes in my metabolism as I get older.)

- What is the underlying motivation? (I want to learn how to better feed and move my body at this stage in my life.)

- Are you enthused to spend your time and energy on it? (I know there isn't a life hack that will help me stay fit as I get older and I want to learn how to help myself stay healthy in the long-term in an enjoyable way, which for me is trail running.)

- What are the mental, emotional, spiritual, physical benefits of attaining this? (I know I will feel better physically, but I believe the benefits of eating better and moving more will positively impact my stress levels, sleep patterns and overall level of tranquility.)

- Keep the intentions short term and fluid enough to evolve and grow.

My wellness intention is:

_____

_____

(to train for my first ultramarathon in November)

David was a colleague I would see once a year at a professional conference. Our careers took a similar arc and, at one point, we were both responsible for global teams in our respective companies. As his career excelled, David struggled to find time for himself, especially when it came to his own wellness practices.

Over coffee during a conference break, David shared his frustration about his sedentary lifestyle.

"Why is it important for you to be more active," I asked.

"Well, I want to get back in shape," he said.

"And how will being in shape impact your life?"

"It will give me more energy."

"That's great," I confirmed. "How do you anticipate your life changing once you have more energy?"

This conversation went on for a bit with me probing on the "Why" while he thought about how his life would be different as a result of the changes he was looking to implement. It wasn't until we were almost leaving the café that we hit on his true motivation.

David leaned over and confided, "While I feel capable, effective and influential at work, the truth is I feel insignificant in the world, almost invisible as I get older. I want to feel energized and enthusiastic about life again."

Ah, now we were getting somewhere…

If David had ended the conversation simply with a goal to go to the gym three times a week, his chances of long-term success would have been low. There would have been nothing to support him when he felt too tired to work out or when he felt embarrassed by his level of fitness as compared to those around him in the gym. But by taking time to think deeply about his "Why," David's original goal of going the gym three times a week turned into a heartfelt intention of living with energy and enthusiasm.

The next time I saw David, he had a twinkle in his eye I had never seen before, along with a lightness in his step. I couldn't wait to hear what he'd done differently in the six months since I saw him last.

"Probably the biggest shift was connecting with how I would feel over time if I continued to show up for my workouts," David reported. "That said," he continued, "most mornings I didn't want to get out of bed an hour earlier and face the gym. But I kept remembering how good it felt to be energized after my workouts. When the alarm went off in the mornings, I focused on wanting to feel that feeling again."

David also confided that he did some writing on the tablet he always carried to take notes during work meetings. He made a dedicated page in the Notes section to jot down his personal thoughts, sometimes during lunch or at meetings when no one knew he was actually working on his personal goals. David recorded all those times when he felt his desired feelings, such as when he had the extra energy to play with his kids on the weekends or when a co-worker paid him a compliment. Recording these changes gave him the motivation to move forward and create more of his desired feelings.

"There are mornings I sleep in, especially when I have a string of late nights due to project deadlines," David confided, "and I've given myself permission to miss a workout here and there. But I have a rule not to miss two in a row. I'm in this for the long run. Rather than perfection, I'm looking to take consistent steps to integrate healthy choices into my lifestyle – I want to continue to feel this level of energy and enthusiasm!"

There's a reason why David experienced such a shift. He connected deeply with how he wanted to feel, and *why*.

"Knowing how you actually want to feel is the most potent form of clarity that you can have. Generating those feelings is the most creative thing you can do with your life." – Danielle LaPorte

The first time I read that quote, it felt like an awakening. Up to that point, I was a goal-driven person, dutifully ticking off one thing after another on my well-structured to-do list. I never thought about how I wanted to feel in relation to what I desired in life.

That all changed when I headed to a warm climate over the December holiday break in 2012 with *The Desire Map* by Danielle LaPorte tucked in my carry-on. Under the Florida Keys sun, I spent several days thinking about my core desired feelings and mapping out activities that would make me feel that way. By the end of that trip, I vowed never to set goals again. I had dug to the underbelly of my "Why" and it was the beginning of my intention setting practice.

Here's how I went about the process:

- I identified five areas of my life that were core for me:
  - Creative Livelihood
  - Intuitive Well-being
  - Relationships – Partnership
  - Relationships – Community (Tribe)
  - Abundant Flow

- To find a related feeling for each area, I asked myself a series of questions:

  - **Creative Livelihood:** Who do I want to be in the world? What makes me feel alive and lights me up? What do I want to learn? How do I want to spend my time? How do I want to feel while working each day? What behaviors no longer serve me?

  - **Intuitive Well-being:** What does wellness look like for me at midlife? How do I nurture my mind, body and spirit? What do I need to change to honor and enhance my vitality?

  - **Relationships – Partnership & Community (Tribe):** What values are key in relationship? How do I want to feel with another? How can I show up for another? How do I participate in my professional and personal communities? What boundaries/discernment are necessary? How can I be of service?

  - **Abundant Flow:** What are my mindset and beliefs around universal flow? Where would I like my finances to be one, five, ten years from now? What behaviors would move me closer to that vision? How can I let life work its magic through me?

The results of the exercise were:

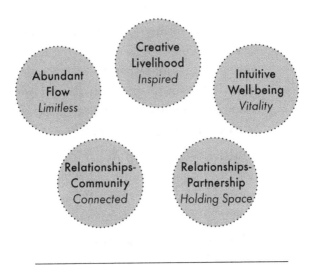

"When I began to think of my work life outside of my corporate frame of reference, I knew I wanted to feel inspired and creative each day. I tried a variety of activities that made me feel that way."

These life areas and related desired feelings have served me well, guiding my actions and behaviors ever since. For example, when I began to think of my work life outside of my corporate frame of reference, I knew I wanted to feel inspired and creative each day. I tried a variety of activities that made me feel that way, such as writing a manuscript and a creative non-fiction blog.

At the same time, I noticed how much I loved learning and experimenting with wellness activities. I started participating in endurance sports in my fifties and enrolled in two sports nutrition classes.

This led to learning more about how to manage my sports performance through food intake. This, in turn, became a passion that led me to wellness coaching and, ultimately, creating the Athena Wellness brand, which inspires me every day. But it started with me wanting to learn how to optimize my own wellness at midlife!

This did not unfold instantly and seamlessly – I did not wake up one morning feeling my desired feelings every day. Adversity was definitely part of the equation.

Things won't always go as planned due to time constraints, the needs of others, travel, injury or family commitments. However, there are ways to anticipate and work through obstacles:

- Develop several implementation intentions to have in your back pocket should you veer off-course. Implementation intentions are *If/Then* statements that help avoid possible obstacles. (*If* I need to work overtime, *then* I'll do my research during my lunch hour.)

- Elicit help from key supporters, working with family and friends so they are clear on what you need, especially in tough times. (When I'm working on my nutrition goals, it would be great to enjoy a brown bag lunch outdoors with healthy food instead of going out to lunch.)

- Check-in daily during your mindfulness practice, morning commute, or your notebook. Play with life questions: What do I want life to look like and why? What will life be like when it happens? What new experiences do I want to have?

- During your daily check-ins, give yourself permission to misstep. Vent your frustrations in your notebook to ease the emotion and look for the lessons in the situation. Take a needed day off or recalibrate, but keep going, especially when encountering roadblocks.

- Utilize intention reminders via Post-it notes, images, and calendar or phone prompts. In the evenings, you can also use your notebook to jot down things that happened in alignment with your intention during the day.

Be flexible and realize there are a variety of routes to get to your intended outcome.

I took multiple paths in working toward my intention to develop a creative livelihood. I didn't stumble on one answer that worked for me, rather I continued to develop a number of approaches that I use at different times. For example, I spent years honing my writing skills, experimenting with different workout routines, trying different nutrition approaches, taking online courses, reading lots of books and getting the training I needed in coaching and business to increase my chances of success.

Intentions ("Why") are seeds of creation, providing clarity to point you in the right direction to attain what you most desire. They allow you to focus on what matters most and release what no longer serves to make space for what's on its way to you.

Intentions do not have to be grand. You can create how you want to feel when you wake, go to work, spend time with your family and friends, contribute to the community, nurture yourself and lay your head down at night. Conversely, you can dream big and act in accordance with your deepest desires and emulate the qualities you admire. This is a fluid and ongoing process.

> **My wellness intention**
> **and related desired feeling:**
>
> _____
> _____

You can live deliberately and authentically, gently moving toward the person you want to become, enjoying the journey as much as the destination.

principle #2:

intention

Writing Practice
....
Conducting a Life Audit

A life audit is a periodic self-reflective exercise to ensure you're living in alignment with your deepest desires.

Try this:

- In your notebook, write your wellness intention and related desired feeling.

- Keep the Role Deconstruction exercise you completed in Chapter Three handy for a point of reference.

- Make a list of activities and time needed to realize your intention. For example, when my intention was to become a coach and feel inspired, I needed to find a wellness coaching program, complete the coursework, arrange my onsite fieldwork, schedule these commitments on my calendar, etc.

- Create two side-by-side lists of how you currently spend your time (work, relationships, hobbies, entertainment, fitness, etc.) and the activities that will move you closer to your wellness intention and desired feeling.

- In your notebook, do a free-writing exercise on some adjustments that can be made to narrow the gap from where you are to where you'd like to be. For example, where can you say no? Are there activities you can scale back or scale up? If you feel like you're holding yourself back in some way, consider dialoguing with your beliefs, values and desired feelings for additional insight.

- Extra credit: Repeat the process for other areas in your life, such as relationships, fitness, or livelihood.

- Alternative writing prompt: If I felt connected to myself, my self-care and self-expression would look like...

Meditation Practice
Intentions and Desired Feelings Visualization

One of the benefits of setting intentions instead of goals is the positive emotions intentions invoke. This practice allows you to envision how realizing the intention will feel.

Try this:

- Close your eyes and take a few deep breaths to ground yourself.

- Bring your intention to mind.

- Imagine how it will feel when your intention comes to fruition:

- What are you doing?

- How do you feel?

- What do you see, smell, taste, hear?

- What makes you motivated and excited?

- Do you feel empowered mentally, physically, emotionally and spiritually?

- How do you look?

- What has changed in your environment?

• Think of three scenarios that you will enjoy once your intention is realized. For example, when I was thinking about starting my business, I envisioned: 1) my book as a best seller; 2) being interviewed on podcasts and television and meeting new colleagues in the wellness space; and 3) coaching, speaking and facilitating workshops that help corporate leaders optimize their well-being. This helped me feel the excitement and freedom of my new life. It also gave me the ability to tap into those feelings to get me through challenges prior to any tangible change in my life.

• In addition to thinking about the future, recall a time when you've had similar achievements or received the assistance you've needed. For example, I drew upon the times I spoke at professional conferences or served as a mentor in my corporate life as a way of welcoming speaking and coaching opportunities as a wellness coach.

• Jot down anything in your notebook that will help you when you encounter resistance or adversity. End with a note of gratitude for all the support you have and will receive.

Positive Action Practice

Wellness Dates

A wellness date is a recurring appointment with yourself for a set period of time dedicated to a nurturing activity. The wellness date is inspired by the artist date popularized by author Julia Cameron in her classic 1990s book on creativity called *The Artist's Way*.

Try this:

- Schedule time each week (ideally), bi-monthly or monthly to enjoy an activity related to your intention that will feel nurturing to you.

- Plan to spend the time alone and unplugged.

- Examples of wellness dates are endless, but here are a few to get you started: taking a nature walk, embarking on a solo road trip, reading, gardening, getting a massage, sleeping in, creating a playlist that evokes your intention-related feelings, journaling in a café, having a healthy meal, simplifying a routine or place in your home, volunteering, playing.

- Keep your wellness dates booked on your calendar and honor the appointment as you would if it were a professional or family commitment.

principle #2:

intention

- There is a difference between goals and intentions, with the latter being rooted in the present and aligned with beliefs and values.

- The "Why" behind behavioral change helps to identify what's at stake if the change isn't implemented.

- Linking the "Why" to desired feelings (why I want it, how it will feel when I get it) provides daily motivation and fuel in times of adversity.

- In your carry-on:
  - Your "Why" as purpose and motivation
  - Life audit analysis
  - Intention and related desired feeling visualization
  - Wellness date

chapter 6

principle #3:

consistency

The art of staying committed and engaged
throughout, especially during challenging times.

Perhaps you've heard the stories. An NFL coach arrives at the playing facility on a July 4th holiday to find his all-star running back doing drills and running stadium steps all by himself. Or the NBA superstar who was in the gym shooting baskets the morning after winning an NBA championship. Or the infamous anti-inflammatory nutrition and flexibility protocols a celebrity quarterback follows year-round that extended his playing career into his forties.

This type of preparation exists in the business world as well, with corporate executives (this author included) overpreparing for important meetings and practicing presentations repeatedly, aloud and in front of the mirror, years into a career, to build the confidence needed to take command in the board room.

The common thread weaving through each of these stories is the importance of consistent action, a critical factor in determining success because it leads to reliable outcomes and results. The reverse is true as well – inconsistent action usually equates to less-than-optimal results.

Why is consistency so impactful? Repetition creates an environment of continuous improvement where feedback and learning can be applied allowing adjustments to be made in real time while moving toward the intended outcome. This trial-and-error approach builds trust with our inner knowing and develops new habits we begin to rely upon. As we continue with consistent practice, our level of personal empowerment also increases because we realize that the responsibility for a beneficial outcome lies within us, leaving little room for blame or excuse.

The more we practice consistency, the more we come to know that being present each day is the key to moving closer to realizing our intentions. With consistent effort, we notice it becomes easier to bypass distractions and immediate gratification in favor of crafting a lifestyle that supports good habits and making the right wellness choices over the long-term.

Momentum builds when we understand that true satisfaction comes from incremental, deliberate choices linked to desired behaviors. We begin embracing the process and the work that is moving us toward our desires.

What determines the degree to which your intentions come to fruition? It depends on the level of energy you consistently apply. Consistent preparation, effort, learning and adjustment are the driving forces of the whole wellness equation – it's how you choose to show up for yourself.

As already noted, great leaps of effort are not required to begin to move toward your intentions. In fact, studies have shown that small steps taken consistently lead to lasting change. Plan to start your wellness efforts with a series of micro-actions. Before long, you'll feel the momentum build and know when you're ready to increase the frequency and intensity of your actions.

So how do you begin to put consistency into actionable practice? Start by revisiting the intention you set when working through the last chapter. Here's a simple format:

- Break the intention down into daily, weekly and monthly micro-actions.

- Write these small actions in your notebook and schedule them in your calendar.

- Organize the necessary resources to get started, including identifying what kind of support you'll need from family and friends.

For example, let's say a businessman named Matt wants to start working out for 30 minutes a day, five days a week, which is at the lower end of the US government guideline range of 150-300 minutes of moderate activity a week.

Matt wants to start exercising because his daughter asked if they could spend her 16th birthday hiking at the Grand Canyon next year (his "Why"). Since Matt is just starting to get back into shape, he decided on brisk morning walks while wearing a simple watch monitor to track his mileage and heart rate.

This is a doable plan. Matt has an activity objective that is attainable at his current fitness level and an intention that's important to him. It's a great way to begin building a foundation that can expand both in time (moving toward 300 minutes of activity a week) and intensity (from walking to jogging to running and/or cross-training).

After a short while, Matt felt recharged and he began to add movement throughout the day, such as taking the stairs and parking his car further away from his destination. He also developed a Plan B to make sure he exercised even when feeling time-crunched. He gives himself the option to break his 30-minute workouts into three 10-minute or two 15-minute sessions, when needed.

Over the months as Matt became fitter, he decided to shake it up with a more rigorous challenge and signed up for his first 5K run. He's currently following a workout plan so he can finish in 30 minutes. He has his eye on a 10K next year and is even considering exploring cross-training with a longer-term goal of participating in a Spartan race one day. The fact that he's even planning for such events has energized Matt. Each day he moves farther away from his sedentary past and makes a commitment toward his active lifestyle and hiking with his family.

Now it's your turn. Bring your wellness intention to mind. Spend a little time reflecting on the result of the Life Audit exercise you completed in Chapter Five. Where are you in relation to where you'd like to be? What are your expectations and what's your available time commitment? How might you begin to move from a basic wellness level toward an optimal one? Use the checklist below to begin to craft a suitable approach of consistent action.

#	Consistency Checklist	✓
1	Review your wellness intention and Life Audit results to determine your area of focus	
2	Begin where you are, with a realistic view of your current circumstances, ability and time commitment – be mindful not to overcommit at first	
3	Select a suitable first step or micro-action (activity)	
4	Connect your activity with your "Why," focusing on the benefit and additive value this action will bring to your life	
5	Create routines to make taking action easier (e.g., a start date, calendar appointment, preparing a gym bag the evening before)	
6	Pay attention to the inner critic and have a plan to combat a negative talk track	
7	Anticipate and clear your biggest obstacles	
8	Share plans with friends, say your intention out loud as extra incentive not to hit the snooze button in the morning	
9	Track progress in your notebook so it's visible and tangible	

Making Consistency the New Norm

In 2013, I had the good fortune to spend a retreat weekend led by fitness guru, Tony Horton, the creator of the P90X home fitness program. Tony is a strong believer in consistency. "Be consistent about being consistent," is one of his many mantras.

During one of the Q&A sessions that weekend, a participant told Tony that his fitness level had plateaued.

"How many times are you working out a week?" Tony asked.

The response was three times a week.

Tony replied, "Working out three times a week is like throwing yourself down a flight of stairs, you'll get sore with little benefit." He recommended a minimum of five times a week with six being optimal and seven possible if it's done correctly through cross-training. Tony's point was that consistency is what builds healthy habits that are integrated into one's lifestyle rather than sporadic activity that leaves you open to bargaining on whether or not to do it.

Part of the reason I've been able to participate in endurance sports well into my fifties is because I schedule workouts for each day of the week, varying the activity, length and intensity. Schedule permitting, I will work out seven days a week, but aspire to a minimum of five and consistently achieve six. I give myself bonus points for additional afternoon walks. I also give myself permission to take days off when I travel extensively or my body signals I need a rest day.

Remember: wellness is a journey, not a destination; it's a way of life that will ebb and flow. The overall aim is to make healthy choices the norm over time, not the exception or something you have to do.

Here are some ideas to help make wellness the norm:

- Immerse yourself in your new activity by learning about it, reading, listening to podcasts, meeting others with the same interests and having fun discovering new things together.

- Be true to yourself rather than fitting in with someone else's wellness expectations and implement changes that matter most to you. What changes will make you feel good and are actionable for you at this time?

- During the first four weeks of a new activity, try not to make exceptions to your workout schedule. Instead, to the extent possible, get into a solid groove.

- On the days you're not feeling motivated, perform your activity anyway. A substandard effort is better than none at all, especially in the beginning.

- Wellness choices do not need to be categorized as good or bad, checked-off or missed. Instead, view choices as those that are right for that day and moment and choose mindfully.

True long-term success is not about perfection. Our best plans can go awry. The key is getting back on track as soon as possible and using the feeling of being off-course to adjust and move forward.

Small achievements can lead to large accomplishments. With enough practice, you will reach a tipping point where things get easier with less mental and emotional effort. Wellness becomes the norm when you keep upgrading your lifestyle, little by little, expecting more of yourself over time, while gradually moving your wellness target forward at periodic intervals.

Strategies to Overcome Resistance

From beginners to pro athletes, everyone faces resistance from time to time. Resistance is anything that prevents us from maintaining a healthy level of wellness and generally falls into two categories, external and internal. Both can take you off-course but you can proactively anticipate and plan for it by determining the source of the resistance and creating strategies to address the obstacle.

External Resistance

- **Definition:** Environmental or physical obstacles
- **Examples:** No access to gym or physical injury
- **Alternatives:** Home workouts (P90X, treadmill) or cross-training (running to keep in shape while rehabbing a shoulder injury)

Internal Resistance

- **Definition:** Excuses or justifications
- **Examples:** Work schedule, family commitments, feeling out of place in the gym
- **Alternatives:** Segment workouts into shorter time periods, involve family members in the activity, begin workouts at home

Of the two types of obstacles, external resistance is easier to address because the solution is usually logistical, such as addressing scheduling issues or adjusting workout plans. Internal resistance is more complex, as it usually stems from thoughts and feelings deep within.

Internal excuses typically take some form of "I don't want to" or "I don't feel like it." Sometimes this is due to fatigue and can be addressed by taking a well-deserved break. But many times, it can be deep-seated, perhaps stemming from an experience that left you feeling judged and vulnerable, like being picked last for a childhood team.

Too many "I don't want tos" and "I don't feel like its" can add up and derail a new wellness routine, especially when we feel frustrated or unmotivated. We can overcome this inertia by unpacking these excuses to see if there's a valid reason for the resistance, such as a limiting belief (not feeling deserving) or unconscious habit (putting the needs of others before your own).

Other feelings that can turn into resistance include feeling awkward from being out of shape or the fear of failure when trying something new, as our protection mechanism works overtime to keep us safe, comfortable and in control. The antidote to these fears is taking small steps to keep change incremental, achievable and less overwhelming.

Keep in mind that you can work with resistance if you practice moving toward it instead of negotiating with it when you feel discomfort. Much like David and Matt experienced, pushing through the lure of sleeping through a scheduled workout can be tempting. When in doubt, always go back to your "Why."

Where the Magic Happens

We have a saying at my boot camp gym. Somewhere toward the end of an hour-long session, when we're running on fumes and counting down the last minutes of the workout, someone (okay, usually me) will shout out, "This is where the magic happens!" It's our reminder to leave it all on the turf we've been pounding for the last 60 minutes. It's our collective cue to empty the tank, because we know that real change happens outside of our comfort zone.

It's also one of the things I've come to love about boot camp workouts and more recently CrossFit. It's always humbling to bump up against a new edge and find a way past what seemed to be a limitation, like climbing a rope for the first time.

David Goggins, a former Navy SEAL turned ultrarunner and motivational speaker, lives by The 40% Rule. He believes that when you're at the point of exhaustion and feel you can't go any further, you're only at 40% of your capacity.

I've experienced this myself and with my clients. It's our mind, not our body or external situations, that gets in our way. What a benefit it is to know that there's always an available supply of energy to support us when we're feeling depleted long before we can see the finish line. The more you push through your perceived limitations, the better you'll understand the depth of your untapped resources.

Minding the Gap (of Change)

At different times during my wellness journey, I have experienced the "gap of change," the in-between place when I was developing healthier habits but still tempted when the old ways came calling.

The gap of change is a place akin to No Woman's Land, uninhabited territory where you can feel tentative and unsupported when taking new steps forward. It's also a confusing place because it's unclear what to let go of and what to build upon. It can feel like living in a sea of uncertainty where the status quo of comfort can be a strong pull back into old habits.

"How do you move through the gap and not get stuck by the fear of moving into the unknown? Having a strong "Why" will help in difficult or tempting situations. "

When I first began taking better care of myself in my mid-thirties, I had to redesign my social life, which, at that time, revolved around regular alcohol consumption, unhealthy food choices and limited sleep. When I began working out and eating clean, it put a strain on my social activities.

Although it wasn't my intention, my lifestyle changes inadvertently shed light on my friend's habits, which eventually led to changes in how I spent my time and with whom. Although uncomfortable at the time, the reprioritization moved me toward my desired intentions.

How do you move through the gap and not get stuck by the fear of moving into the unknown? Having a strong "Why" will help in difficult or tempting situations. Continuously connecting to the positive emotion behind what you desire fuels your transformation efforts.

There are plenty of people who would love to be part of your healthy support group. In fact, you may even inspire those around you to change when the time is right for them and join your expanding community that prioritizes practices that increase mind, body and spiritual well-being.

Creating a Lifestyle that Supports Good Habits

Prioritizing Yourself

Consistent action is a way for you to make yourself a priority and give yourself permission to spend time on activities that increase self-care, you enjoy, or are curious to learn more about. If you feel a twinge of guilt in reading those words, remind yourself how you consistently show up for others, including your work, family, friends and community. Wellness starts by adding yourself to the list.

Creating long-term change takes time. Truth be told, there are days when I still think about ways to get out of my workouts when my early morning alarm sounds. I find myself mentally reviewing the day's calendar to figure out if I can sleep in and exercise later. But, after all these years, I rarely give in to the negotiation. Instead, I think of how good it will feel to have the workout behind me, to feel my blood flow, to see my friends I know are waiting for me at the gym.

You can apply the same techniques to your wellness challenges. What would it be like to choose to be mindful throughout the day, or feel your blood flowing through movement, or be emotionally non-reactive when something doesn't go as planned?

These choices are additive. After a morning session of meditation or exercise, you may begin to crave healthy food to keep your metabolism up. You may look forward to feeling sore the day after a hard workout, knowing you put in good effort. Perhaps you can catch yourself before responding when someone cuts you off on the highway. You will likely feel the positive effect of putting yourself first in other parts of your life, as well.

Thriving with Seasonality

You may also choose to use the power of our natural cycles to boost your wellness routines, as energy naturally ebbs and flows with the seasons. For example, you may tend toward more aerobic activity in the summer, choosing to run outside instead of on the treadmill, eating more fruit and salad, and being more social. Conversely, in the winter, you may incorporate more weight workouts, eat more grains and soups and focus more inwardly.

Wellness by Subtraction

If you want to make wellness changes but, at the moment, are scheduled to the hilt, don't forget there is also the consistent choice to not doing something. What if wellness could be impacted by stopping something you're doing instead of adding a new practice? Or what if you could add spaciousness to your day by intentionally pausing for a short period of time?

At the height of my corporate career, there were times where I felt, despite my best efforts, that I could not keep up with everyone's demands and expectations. This left me feeling tired upon waking and unable to conjure up the willpower to add one more thing to my pile of tasks.

Back then what I needed most was to make space for myself. Since time was a limited and precious commodity, I couldn't carve out significant periods of time to optimize my wellness. So, I started with just a few minutes at a time – five minutes first thing every morning where I had no decisions to make and nothing to do in that moment.

Once I began to enjoy and rely on having time that was completely mine (five minutes upon waking, breathing deeply with my hand over my heart), I noticed I began to want more time in that place. That's what ultimately led me to a more formal meditation practice that has continuously evolved and paid dividends over the years. But it started with just five minutes.

Other examples of what you could stop doing to improve your wellness include:

- **Try intermittent fasting** – Concentrating your meal intake to shortened periods of time, such as from 10 a.m. to 6 p.m. You may find when you practice this technique, the time spent shopping and preparing food significantly declines.

- **Reduce alcohol consumption** – Aside from the known health risks of drinking (heart and liver damage), you may find you sleep better and have more energy in the mornings if you decide not to drink alcohol.

- **Practice under-scheduling** – It's natural for the overscheduled to raise their hands to volunteer whenever asked. Once you begin to enjoy small, intentional pauses, you may find yourself assessing the impact of saying "yes" even though you'd rather not participate.

You can explore the wellness possibilities of not doing something by asking yourself what you can subtract from your routine that would add vitality to your life. It could be something you're eating or drinking (sugar), places you're devoting your time with little payback (volunteering for an extra work project), or an activity that may look like stress relief but is actually contributing to your overscheduled stress (binge-watching a TV series).

Simply knowing you have a choice to pause and make a little space in your life will lead to a more optimistic outlook. Practicing wellness by subtraction is sure to not only add time, but energy and focus to the things that matter most to you.

Opportunity is missed by most people because it is dressed in overalls and looks like work. – Thomas Edison

Thomas Edison is known for his many inventions, including the incandescent light bulb, phonograph, movie camera, film and mimeograph (remember that?!). He held over 1000 patents for his many inventions. The secret for his output was consistency.

Edison logged thousands of experiments and credited that high-volume output with his success rate, once stating, "I have not failed, I've just found 10,000 ways that won't work."

Also a prolific writer, Edison kept detailed journals of his work and life. His 10,000 ways that didn't work were analyzed in his notebooks so he could incorporate prior learning into new experiments. Invention and innovation were his intentions and consistent effort and learning his fuel.

Where intentions meet consistency – that's where the magic happens.

principle #3:

consistency

Writing Practice

Showing Up and Giving Permission to Yourself

This practice is about acknowledging how you're already being consistent in your life while exploring ways to give yourself permission to focus more time on your own self-care.

1. Try this – I am already showing up for myself by…:

- Take out your notebook and write "I am already showing up for myself by…" at the top.

- Set the timer on your phone for 10 minutes.

- Begin listing the ways you are consistently investing in your own self-care. For example, writing in your notebook, meditating, eating a healthy breakfast, working out, getting quality sleep, spending time alone, simplifying your routine, decluttering, etc.

- Whenever you complete a thought, write "I am already showing up for myself by…" and begin again. Keep going until the timer sounds.

- If you listed all the ways you've shown up for

yourself and there's still time left, you can change the lead-in phrase to "I will show up for myself by…"

2. Try this – Granting more permission:

- Using your notebook to brainstorm, think about how you could be more intentional about giving yourself permission to further prioritize your self-care.

- Self-care is broadly defined as the practice of taking deliberate action to nurture your mind, body and spirit. Take a few minutes to define self-care in a meaningful way for yourself.

- Now list a few benefits of your self-care that are most critical for you. For example, are your practices helping you stave off burnout, as they did for me in my thirties? Do your practices provide much needed alone time, as my first long trail runs did in my forties? Perhaps you love being part of a broader community, as I do now with my boot camp and CrossFit friends.

- Brainstorm ways to further prioritize your self-care time – remember to be kind to yourself as you work through the list:

  - Can you schedule self-care time first as you plan your week?

  - Are there social activities you need to decline?

  - Are there household or work activities you can delegate?

- Can you make your self-care appointments non-negotiable?

- Are you doing things you don't want to do or that are not in line with your intentions?

- Can you ask for help?

- Do you know your limits and boundaries and are you honoring them?

• Dialogue with any resistance or old thought patterns.

• To enjoy pure "me time," once a week schedule in something that feels decadent and luxurious to you:

  - Buy yourself flowers

  - Unplug for a specific amount of time

  - Take a nap, go to bed early or sleep in late

  - Watch your favorite movie

  - Learn or try something new and uncharacteristic

  - Prepare a healthy meal

  - Book a massage

  - Trust your inner knowing

  - Give 100% effort instead of 150% (and use that additional time for yourself)

  - Give yourself permission to do nothing

Meditation Practice

Future Self Visualization

Many of us can quickly identify the voice of the Inner Critic, but it takes some practice to connect with and rely on our Inner Coach. The following is an adaptation of a visualization exercise developed by the Coaches Training Institute. I have found this exercise invaluable to transcend limiting beliefs and familiar boundaries. You may choose to record the following steps or search for a similar visualization online.

Try this:

- Close your eyes and take a few deep breaths to ground yourself.

- Imagine yourself being transported upward – past your home, town, country, into the darkness of outer space, where you can see the earth's curve, hear the silence and feel the cool air around you.

- Notice a beam of light and follow it back down to earth. This beam is taking you 20 years into the future.

- Take a look around you and notice the dwelling that's in front of you. It belongs to your Future Self.

- Note the following:

  - Where are you? What's the landscape like? What does the house look like?

- Knock on the door. What does your Future Self look like? How does she greet you? What is she wearing? How does her essence feel?

- Where does she take you to have a conversation? How does the interior of her home feel?

- What does she offer you to eat and drink?

- Ask her: What stands out the most from these last 20 years?

- Ask her: How do I get from where I am to where you are?

- Ask her any other question you'd like.

- Notice that she has a gift for you. It could be an object, word, image, metaphor or symbol.

- Thank your Future Self for her gift, time and wisdom.

- As you leave her home, know you can return any time.

• Travel back up the light beam into outer space. When you step off, gently float back to your present time and space, feeling grounded, alert and refreshed.

• Spend 10 minutes writing about your experience in your notebook, focusing on your senses and noting any helpful information you learned from your Future Self.

```
┌─────────────────────────────────────────────┐
│            Positive Action Practice           │
│         ·····························          │
│              Future Self Emulation            │
└─────────────────────────────────────────────┘
```

Your Future Self holds valuable clues and can provide fun places for you to explore. Consider finding ways to spend time or handle situations as she would, trying on your future persona a little at a time.

Try this:

- Begin by envisioning different aspects of your Future Self's life. For example:

  - What self-care rituals does she have?

  - How does she nurture her mind, body and spirit?

  - How does she dress?

  - Does she work?

  - What does she eat?

  - How is her home furnished?

  - How does she handle difficult situations?

  - What are her relationships like?

  - How does she handle her finances?

  - What does she do for fun?

- Each week as you're scheduling in your self-care, have some fun "acting as if" you were your Future Self. Enjoy a meal, dress, spend time, handle a situation or nurture yourself as she would.

principle #3:

consistency

- Consistent action leads to reliable and successful outcomes.

- There's magic in the combination of intention and consistency.

- There are strategies to overcome resistance.

- The gap of change can be difficult to navigate.

- Creating a lifestyle that supports healthy habits is the end goal.

- In your carry-on:

    - Consistency checklist

    - Ways you're showing up for yourself and granting permission for further nurturing

    - Your Future Self as a mentor

    - Emulating your Future Self

chapter 7

principle #4:
growth mindset

How you view the wellness journey ahead will determine your progress and enjoyment. Applying a growth mindset where challenges are seen as opportunities will position you to move forward with grace and ease.

I vividly remember my first boot camp class a few years ago. I had just moved and wanted to meet people in my new town while getting in my workouts. During my first session, I was surprised by the degree of intensity of some of the moves, like wall walks, burpees and rope slams. The pace felt relentless and when I finally got home at 7 a.m., I turned on the coffee pot and collapsed on the couch for 15 minutes before dragging myself to the shower to get ready for work.

When the alarm went off the next morning and I reached toward my night table to shut it off, I was jolted by the level of soreness I felt. "Uh-oh," I groaned as I laid there and did a body scan realizing that every single muscle in my body ached. I could barely get out of bed. For the next five days, each time I got out of my car or up from my desk, my quads would freeze for a minute. I would wince and breathe deeply before taking a step.

But when the following Monday came, I was out of bed by 4:45 a.m. and in the gym by 5:30 a.m., nervously awaiting the first round of instructions. Based on my first experience, I knew I'd find a way to make it through the workout, although at the end of 60 minutes my energy was fully depleted.

"This is how a growth mindset works. By choosing to focus our energy and resources on the positive, instead of focusing on the negative, we take ownership of our emotions and experiences."

Over the next few weeks, I felt a little more energy toward the end of the workout and a little less sore afterward. Some days the improvement was barely noticeable, but, in hindsight, the boot camp workouts did get easier over time. Even so, these workouts were something I endured rather than enjoyed.

Something significantly shifted after a year of training. I began to appreciate certain aspects of the workouts, such as my ability to handle the unpredictability of the routines and how I could feel the blood pumping through my body as I moved around the gym. I began to equate the once uncomfortable burn I felt in my muscles with being alive and strong rather than fatigued. I began to appreciate my body for what it could do, which was a lot for a 50+-year-old woman. I also reconnected with my "Why," including the sense of community I felt working out with my new friends.

That mindset reframe served me well. Working out no longer felt like something I *had* to do – it became something I *got* to do.

This is how a growth mindset works. By choosing to focus our energy and resources on the positive, instead of focusing on the negative, we take ownership of our emotions and experiences.

When you adopt a growth mindset, you begin to increase your focus on what is right in your life. The more you practice this mindset, the more you'll begin to experience challenges as opportunities that will position you to gracefully move forward.

There are two components in the dictionary definition of mindset:

1. A fixed mental *attitude* or disposition that predetermines a person's responses to and interpretations of situations.

2. An inclination or *habit*.

What do mindset, attitude and habits have to do with our health, fitness level, well-being and overall success in life? Everything! Your attitude is your frame of mind. Your habits create who you are and determine where you're going. Putting your attitude and habits to work within a growth mindset will serve as an accelerator for optimized well-being.

Growth Mindset Equation

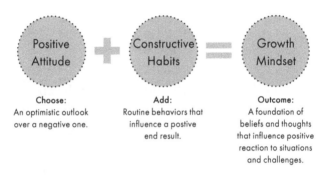

Choose:
An optimistic outlook over a negative one.

Add:
Routine behaviors that influence a postive end result.

Outcome:
A foundation of beliefs and thoughts that influence positive reaction to situations and challenges.

The Two Components of Mindset

Attitude

A positive attitude is a state of mind that has the capacity to envision and routinely expect favorable outcomes, which influences behavior. A person with a positive attitude:

- Builds on a foundation of optimism and positive thinking

- Views situations positively (I can, we will, it's

possible) and does not contribute to fear-based thinking or actions

- Perceives obstacles as opportunistic challenges
- Acknowledges but does not dwell on problems and sees the silver lining in the unexpected
- Tries new things
- Appreciates the virtuous in all people and believes in a greater good for all
- Accepts the world as it is and works to make it better.

Do you have a love/hate relationship with your wellness practice? Do you find yourself "rubber-banding" back and forth between positive thoughts and the absence of them? Since your mindset is comprised of thoughts that influence attitude, shifting those thoughts can quite literally change your life.

Sometimes just a small shift in attitude can get you going in the right direction. For example, forcing yourself to the gym and going through the motions of a workout through sheer will only works for so long. Here's how changing your thoughts can shift the feeling from drudgery to being open to trying something new:

Old thought: "I don't want to go to the gym."

New thought: "I haven't found an exercise I enjoy *yet*, but maybe I can take a small actionable step toward better well-being, even if I don't love it… *yet*. This week I will try ____*(fill-in-the-blank)*____."

You may also find it helpful to ease off on the need for perfection. If you wanted to do an hour-long workout but overslept, 10-15 minutes of movement is still better than nothing, and it keeps you progressing. Over time, regular movement will make a difference. Walking 15 minutes a day, five days a week equals 3,900 minutes or 65 hours of movement a year. It adds up!

Your perspective and mindset can also shift when you rename the challenge you're facing. For example, you may want to work out, eat better and feed your family healthier meals, but you tell yourself you don't have the time. How can you make this work when the story of "I don't have the time" surfaces? Is it actually true? Where can time be found?

When I was training for my ultramarathon, I was working a full-time corporate job, taking care of a household, attending to my relationship and along with my siblings, assisting an aging father who was grieving the recent loss of our mother.

Putting in 25-50 miles a week on top of cross-training workouts could have felt overwhelming. Instead, I changed how I thought about my training to make running my refuge – a block of hours that I had all to myself to process everything that was happening around me. I also used it as time to listen to music or my favorite podcasts or just be fully present and in connection with nature on the trails. It changed my long training runs from something I had to do to an activity

I looked forward to and enjoyed. Running provided relief, release and uplift. Although my wellness activity was based on physical activity, it had a positive impact on my emotional, mental and spiritual well-being.

How can you shift your perspective on an important wellness issue? If time is a struggle, is there someone who can help you with routine activities, such as the grocery shopping or preparing meals? Are there things you're doing that can be put on hold so you can free up the time for wellness activities? Is there a timesaving technique? How can your family get involved?

I have found that when something becomes a priority, your schedule will gradually loosen to make room for it. It takes a bit of planning and some time, but schedules will realign as you commit to your well-being.

There may be times when you're just feeling stuck. Try making a note of what you have right now that you're grateful for – it's a simple technique that alters perspective. For example, if you're feeling time crunched, where do you feel appreciative for the help you have today? Perhaps you have a wonderful assistant or productive team member. Maybe your family or friends have stepped up to help when needed. Being thankful and appreciative for what you already have affirms the goodness in your life. That, in turn, creates an optimistic outlook, which fuels growth.

As noted in Chapter Four, you can create a gratitude practice by writing about the things that are going right in your life. You may be surprised how quickly this practice can shift perspective from one that feels fixed or negative to one that is expansive.

Habit

The second element of a growth mindset is habit, which is defined as something we do regularly, sometimes without thought. I like to think of habit as a groove – a way to make good choices routine and easy by the support system created around it.

People who establish and practice good habits tend to be:

- **Self-motivated and action-oriented** – They rise early, minimize time spent on television and social media, and keep track of appointments and tasks.

- **Disciplined and health conscious** – They eat well, exercise regularly, and prioritize sleep.

- **People-oriented** – They develop healthy relationships, volunteer in their community, and focus on what matters most.

- **Emotionally mature** – They establish boundaries but are generous with time and resources.

- **Growth-oriented** – They invest in practices that support their continuous improvement and ongoing learning.

Of course, some habits can also work against us. We all have unfavorable habits that have become actions we perform on "autopilot." These are done without much thought or consideration as to how they are affecting us long term. These habits may be sabotaging what we really want out of life.

An adverse habit can be something as simple as going to the fast food drive-thru each day because it's on the way home and it's easier than preparing a meal. It could be coming home from work and watching TV, spending time on social media, or numbing out with wine instead of going for a walk or connecting with a loved one. It may be sleeping later each morning instead of waking up to fix a healthy breakfast or prepare lunch to take to work.

What habits have you formed that are in direct conflict with your wellness aspirations?

Going back to my ultramarathon example, I had to find a way to make training a priority for five months. I did this by scheduling my running mileage and the types of workouts I needed to complete from mid-June to mid-November. Each week I would review what I planned to do and write the specific workouts in my calendar for the next seven days.

In addition, to prepare for longer runs on the weekend, I wrote a list on an index card that included actions I could take the night before and morning of the workout. I laid out my clothes, charged my watch and prepared food and drink in the evening so I could pack the cooler and get on the trails early the next day.

Since I needed my rest, many of my Friday and Saturday evening plans shifted from social time to early curfews. After a few weeks of intentionally planning in this manner, my social activities naturally shifted toward supporting my workouts, such as running in the park with a friend and talking in a local juice bar afterward.

Without realizing it, I was following a pattern that behavioral psychologists use to encourage forming good habits:

- **Routine** – I documented the actions I needed to take on an index card to make the preparation for my long runs memorable and easy to perform.

- **Cues** – The visual reminders and the act of laying out my clothes and preparing my food got me in the frame of mind for the long run.

- **Incentive** – The behavior of sticking with my training plan was reinforced with a reward each time I reached a new milestone, usually in the form of a massage, rest day or celebratory meal with loved ones. I also made sure I gave myself things to look forward to, such as a new route to explore or an interesting podcast on a new topic.

The secret of forming good habits starts with the awareness that seemingly small or inconsequential decisions you make add up over time. This can be detrimental if you're making decisions in conflict with your desires, such as routinely sleeping in instead of working out, but these individual decisions can be monitored and changed as needed. The trajectory of good habits will propel you forward if your decision-making is in alignment with where you want to go.

To summarize, when I think of mindset, I'm reminded of a story attributed to the Cherokee lineage.

An elder is walking with his grandson and talking about life. "A fight is going on inside me," the grandfather says. "It's a terrible fight and it's between two wolves. One is evil – he is anger, sorrow, regret, greed, arrogance, self-pity, guilt, resentment, inferiority, lies, false pride, superiority and ego.

"The other is good – he is joy, peace, love, hope, serenity, humility, kindness, benevolence, empathy, generosity, truth, compassion and faith. The same fight is going on inside you and inside every other person, too."

The grandson gave it some thought and then asked, "Which wolf will win?"

The grandfather replied, "The one you feed."

Attitude and habits are intertwined and play a huge part in who you are and who you will become. Shifts from a fixed mindset of "I should" to a growth mindset of "I will" feeds the good wolf and puts the power back into your hands.

principle #4:
growth mindset

Writing Practice
....
Feeding the Good Wolf

This practice is about acknowledging and expanding the ways you're feeding the good wolf while creating strategies to defend against the bad wolf.

1. Try this – I am creating positive energy by:

- Take out your notebook and write "I am creating positive energy by…" at the top.

- Set the timer on your phone for 10 minutes.

- Begin listing the ways you are already feeding the good wolf. For example, paying it forward by buying coffee for the next person in line, starting a gratitude list in your notebook, writing a mentor a thank-you letter, giving a compliment, spending quality time with loved ones or alone.

- Whenever you complete a thought, write "I am creating positive energy by…" and begin again. Keep going until the timer sounds.

- Alternative writing prompt: Three ways I am feeding (or I can feed) the good wolf include…

2. Try this – Feeding the good wolf:

- What are some of the qualities of your destructive wolf (fixed mindset)? Your good wolf (growth mindset)? What are some ways you can minimize what you feed the destructive one and maximize what gets fed to the good one?

- How do you increase awareness of the times you're operating from a fixed mindset? How can you quickly realign with growth mindset?

- It has been my experience that the bad wolf's insatiable hunger is really my own longing to connect more deeply with myself. How might your self-care practices combat the bad wolf?

Meditation Practice
Smiling Meditation

Buddhist monk Thich Nhat Hanh has published dozens of books and is a proponent of mindfulness and presence. His practices are user-friendly and can be used to briefly pause throughout the day as reminders to breathe, be present, and smile – all food for the good wolf.

Try this:

- Take a deep breath in, hold briefly and exhale. Repeat two more times.

- Be fully present in whatever you're doing – driving, sitting, walking, eating, drinking a cup of tea.

- Repeat a Thich Nhat Hanh-like phrase, such as "Breathing in I calm my body, breathing out I smile," several times.

- Acknowledge the moment of happiness and peace as you direct the smile inward and then outward.

Positive Action Practice

"Raise the Spirit" Repertoire

Over the years I created quite a collection of inspirational resources to keep my good wolf fed and my spirits high, even when my reality was difficult and challenging. My books, music, podcasts, online classes, retreats, activities, exercise, meditation, food, journaling, visualization, affirmations and travels were all geared to keep my energy high and positive.

One of my favorite tools, however, is my digital vision board, filled with images that generate my desired feelings across the Holistic Wellness Spectrum.

Try this – Digital vision board:

- Select a digital picture frame that is equipped with Bluetooth and internet connectivity.

- Collect a mix of personal photos, quotes and images with a focus on how you feel. Keep in mind that you are creating a space that evokes your desired feelings and good vibes to create an inspired mindset.

- Upload your content. Program the frame so the images continuously shuffle and that it runs when you wake (my frame is in my master bath).

- As you watch the slideshow, focus on how you feel. In the expansiveness of possibility, take a moment to feel a sense of gratitude for what brought you to this point while feeling the energy of what's on the horizon.

- Make the slideshow a daily practice. Enjoy the feeling of waking to the images of the life of your dreams. The repetitiveness of the images and related feelings are what makes this process so powerful. It sets the tone for the entire day.

- Keep it fresh. As you come across new images or quotes, upload them to your board. My frame works with an app that makes this process seamless and reflects the dynamic arc of my life.

- Extra credit: Assemble your own "Raise the Spirit" repertoire of inspired multi-media resources (phone, tablet, computer) and use often!

principle #4:

growth mindset

- Mindset can be negative (fixed) or positive (growth).

- The two components of mindset are:

  - Attitude: frame of mind

  - Habit: behaviors that influence results.

- When you choose an optimistic outlook and add constructive habits, the result is a growth mindset.

- A growth mindset is an accelerator for optimized well-being.

- Routines, cues and incentives can be used to reinforce good habits – which all feed "the good wolf."

- In your carry-on:

  - Optimistic attitude

  - Constructive habits

  - Smiling meditation

  - "Raise the Spirit" repertoire, including the digital vision board

chapter
8

principle #5:
accountability

A systematic way to check-in with what you commit to accomplish, celebrate the wins, and compassionately adjust where needed.

Okay, I will admit it. This Principle may not be the sexiest of the five. But accountability is a powerful determinant of whether or not your wellness intentions will be realized.

Accountability sounds like a heavy, burdensome word, but it simply means a willingness to take responsibility for your actions and related consequences. Being accountable to yourself is about follow-through, acknowledging when things don't go as planned, and finding solutions to get back on track.

If accountability is doing what we say we'll do, commitment is the obligation to do it. This includes having the tenacity to keep going when faced with failure and using mistakes as a way to continuously improve.

Remember Hanna, the investment banker we met in Chapter One? At first glance, she thought she needed to make some habit changes to eat better and exercise. Then she noticed how her overscheduled lifestyle didn't feed her soul. She committed to changing how she was spending her time and started a writing practice to explore what it would be like to live a more authentic life.

Nine months into her writing experiment, Hanna experienced some ups and downs when attempting to implement change.

"You know, it would have been easier to just focus on losing ten pounds," she joked.

I asked Hanna what her biggest wellness obstacle had been.

"Over-commitment, hands down," she said.

"How do you handle it?" I asked.

"Over-committing is something I face every day because it's my unconscious default," she said. "I have to constantly remind myself to look at the daily choices I'm making through the lens of my longer-term vision for myself, which is to put my wellness needs first.

"Not over-committing is a daily practice and I don't always get it right. It's like I'm wired to take on more responsibility and have had to learn to proactively weigh the impact of agreeing to something and how I might otherwise use that time. But it sure feels good when I get it right!

"For example, I blocked out the first two appointments in my work calendar and last one in the evenings so meetings cannot be scheduled during that time. This gives me time to start the day in a more measured way and end the day with time to write a to-do list for the next day. I also do not take calls during my commute anymore and now use that time for me, whether it's music, audiobooks, podcasts or silent reflection. I've come to enjoy the process of easing in and out of my day. I actually find I'm more productive during my workday as a result, which is an added bonus!"

Hanna paused in a moment of reflection and then concluded, "I think the biggest surprise, though, is what happens in the quiet moments. It's like hearing little whispers coming from deep within telling me where to look next. It's wordless, more of a feeling or a pull, but I find I'm being drawn to things, like spending time in nature, and I like that. I recently joined a Meetup hiking group I found online. It's been a great way to get exercise and I find I love being outdoors for a few hours early on a Saturday morning with a nice group of folks and sometimes my family joins me. It's very rejuvenating."

Hanna demonstrates many of the qualities that are associated with accountability, including taking ownership of her actions and tending to herself. Little by little, she's finding ways to utilize these qualities to live from a more wholehearted place.

Qualities of Accountability		
Takes responsibility	Ownership of actions	Tends to self
Makes no excuses	Creates boundaries	Self-aware
Puts in effort	Manages expectations	Protects energy
Places no blame	Controls own fate	Owns feelings
Self-motivated	Delivers timely	Collaborates
High integrity	Fixes mistakes	Dependable
Self-reliant	Solves problems	Positive attitude

The core tenets of the Principle of Accountability are *checking in* on your progress, *celebrating wins* and *adjusting* where needed.

Checking In

There are numerous ways to structure your check-in process. At a minimum, you'll need to determine how and when you check-in with yourself. I like to do my check-ins weekly on a Sunday evening. It sets me up for the upcoming week.

I use a weekly planner and my notebook to plan and track my progress against my wellness objectives. I start each session with an honest assessment.

During a week when I'm on track, I give myself kudos for successfully planning and fulfilling my objectives, such as completing my workouts or meditating each day, as well as proactively considering my schedule and commitments. During weeks when things don't go as intended, I review the reasons why, such as a work deadline or business trip, and plan accordingly next time. I try to be as objective as possible and avoid self-blame, shame or criticism.

Here are some things to keep in mind as you structure your process:

- Determine where you'll record your daily progress, such as your notebook or planner, including what you do each day and how you feel.

- Schedule a time to perform the review each week.

- During your weekly review, look for patterns involved in what went well and what didn't. For example, you may find yourself numbing out with late night television, which makes it hard to get up for an early morning workout. Do you feel areas of resistance? Is there anything you can start or stop doing that will move you closer to realizing your intention?

- Note how satisfied you are with your progress, the specific wellness results you achieved, and your level of overall improvement, remembering to give yourself credit for things that go well and practicing non-judgment when things don't go as planned.

Celebrating Wins

Celebrating wellness milestones releases endorphins and reinforces the building of healthy habits. When you celebrate, small victories become associated with good feelings and the body craves more of those feel-good chemicals, which strengthens the habit. In addition, self-efficacy, or the belief that you can accomplish what you set out to do, increases.

Both large and small milestones can be rewarded. Achievements might include a positive change in physical metrics (cholesterol, blood pressure, blood sugar), muscle gain, better fitting clothes, the ability to perform more reps, learning a new skill, taking time to do an activity you love, an increased range of motion, maintaining a meditation streak, practicing better sleep habits, drinking a certain amount of water per day, and/or giving up an unhealthy habit, such as smoking or drinking soda.

The way you choose to reward yourself is up to you. It can be anything that makes you happy, including pursuing a favorite activity (a night out with friends, dancing); attending a special event (concert, movie); giving yourself a physical reward or gift (new sneakers, a book); and/or spending time on a favorite activity (reading, gardening, photography, playing the guitar, being in nature).

Making Adjustments

There may be times when, despite your best efforts, you're not seeing the results you initially envisioned.

Here are some things to consider as you determine next steps:

- How was your effort level? Did you give it your all or can you increase the intensity?

- Were there changes in your situation that impacted your plans, such as a work deadline or a change in the family's schedule, like school spring break? What can be done to realign your schedule and support system?

- Were your expectations too high? Did you try to take too large a step (completely cut sugar out of your diet)? Is it possible to break your task down into smaller actions (replace soda with sparking water to start)? If so, what will be done and by when?

- If you're feeling good, is it possible to continue the effort while being less concerned with the end result?

- Are you still interested in achieving this wellness milestone? It's okay to redirect your energy if you're not all in, as long as it doesn't become a recurring practice.

Accountability Tools, Partners, and Community

Since willpower is a finite resource and stressors can further deplete your intent to stay on track, other techniques can be helpful to keep you accountable, including:

1. utilizing **tools**

2. finding an **accountability partner**

3. joining a **community of interest**

You can mix and match elements from each category to create a support system that works for you to measure, track and adjust your progress. The type of support you choose will depend on your level of self-motivation, your comfort in sharing your plan with others, and your preference for solo or group activities.

1. **Tools** – there are numerous devices to keep you on track, ranging from analog to digital, to help with consistent focus and influence positive results:

- *Planners* can be used to schedule specific activities. I use a combination of a paper planner and electronic calendar. I track all of my appointments, including my workouts.

- *Action logs* can be used to track activity. I use one for exercise. Each December I create a simple grid for each month of the following year using a spreadsheet program. The template includes each day of the month down the left-hand side of the page and columns to track the time of the workout, type of activity, duration of session, number of miles (if applicable), calories burned and intensity level (heart rate or high point). For me, there's something about seeing the entire month on one page – the blank spaces make missed workouts very evident.

Each month, I total the number of workouts I did, the minutes I exercised and the miles I ran. At the end of the year, I total the activity from January to December. I find it motivating to see what was accomplished and a great way to start the new year.

Date	Day	AM/PM	Activity	How Long?	How Far?	Cals Burned	HR/HP
1 Jan	Tue						
2 Jan	Wed						
3 Jan	Thu						
4 Jan	Fri						
5 Jan	Sat						
6 Jan	Sun						
7 Jan	Mon						
...							
31 Jan	Fri						

- *Nutrition logs* can be simple (manually tracking hydration or servings of fruit and vegetables) or more complex (tracking every meal electronically). Keeping a nutrition log was essential for me when I was first learning about portions (a skillset that wasn't innate for an Italian gal) back in my thirties. In recent years, I've used an app when I felt I needed data to make adjustments to my food intake.

- *Year-at-a-Glance calendar* can be used for any daily activity. A story has circulated in writing circles for years about Jerry Seinfeld's use of such a calendar to track his comedy writing sessions. His method to ensure he wrote daily was to display a new calendar each January and make a big red "X" on each day he wrote. His intention was to "never break that chain" and it is quite a visual motivator.

- *Apps* can be used to track nutrition, exercise, sleep and meditation. In addition, there are accountability apps that allow you to set your goal, set the stakes if you fall short (i.e., select a charity that will receive a donation from you), and invite a support group of friends to track you online.

- *Wearable tracking devices*, such as smart watches and fitness trackers, can provide real-time feedback and send data to your apps.

- *Virtual activities*, such as virtual races, have helped me through long New Jersey winters by providing a fitness event (a 10K race) that I could run indoors on my treadmill, upload my results and see how I did in comparison to other runners.

- *Pre-booking and prepaying* for wellness activities, such as a personal training or coaching session, can be effective, knowing someone is expecting your presence or results.

- Using your *notebook* to check-in on how you're feeling about your activity and obstacles is a great way of being accountable for yourself while spending time exploring your inner world.

2. **An accountability partner** – You may choose to work with someone who can hold you to your commitments and provide feedback and support, such as someone in your network or a trainer or coach. If you hire someone, they can also help increase a skill or ability given their expertise and experience. Hired wellness practitioners can also provide tailored programs and goal progress monitoring.

- Accountability relationships can be in person or online and work best when there is:
  - A clear agreement of what is to be accomplished as well as the feedback and support expectations
  - An accountability contract that provides structure, including check-in timing and frequency, discussion topics, and rewards, as well as consequences, if goals aren't reached
  - Familiarity with your wellness objective
  - A positive outlook
  - A high level of trust
  - Comfort to honestly share progress and challenges

- Objectivity to uncover the root cause of obstacles and cut through excuses

- A back-up plan for unanticipated events, like sickness or travel.

• In lieu of a 1:1 accountability partner relationship, you can use:

- Online competitions through trackers and apps (such as Garmin and Strava)

- Exercise equipment with an online component (such as Peloton)

- Social media progress posting

- Public declaration of your commitment, such as letting your work colleagues know about your wellness objectives and activities.

There are pros and cons of publicly sharing your new endeavor, especially if the activity is atypical for you. An obvious advantage to sharing your commitment is that when you tell people, you are more accountable to completing the task you set out to accomplish. Conversely, there is a negative to revealing too much, too soon.

For example, while writing in your notebook, you may have uncovered a long-forgotten dream of being an artist. While your newfound aspiration may be to have your art hanging on a New York City gallery wall someday, it may be too vulnerable to share that long-term vision at an early stage. Rather, you may choose to share with your friends and colleagues that you're taking an evening painting class at a local college.

3. **Communities of interest** – these are in-person or virtual groups that share a common interest and gather to exchange thoughts and ideas on a topic. New connections in the wellness community can provide encouragement, perspective, compatibility, advice, check-ins, shared experiences and stretch goals. Community can be formed through:

- Social media activities, such as online forums and wellness communities (Facebook specialty groups for midlife wellness)

- Friends and workout partners who know your wellness objectives can provide support through calls, texts and in-person meetings

- Connections made through events, such as Cycle for the Cause, or community events, such as a local mini-triathlon or 5K run

- Group activities, such as boot camp or CrossFit

- Meetup events

- Wellness or meditation retreats and gatherings at retreat locations like Omega Institute in New York, Kripalu in Massachusetts, and 1440 and Esalen in California.

The people we associate with influence our habits, both good and bad. Having a solid support system helps to lock in our accountability commitment and builds a sense of belonging.

Being accountable to yourself for what you really want is an empowering way to live. Your personal power will get a boost every time you own a success or a mistake, when you pause to celebrate a milestone,

"You are the result of all the daily decisions you make. "

or when you adjust your plan and move forward on the path you're carving out for yourself. By doing so, your self-trust increases as does your ability to model the positive behavior for others.

You are the result of all the daily decisions you make. Put another way, every day you are actively creating the person you will become. Are you living your truth? Are you giving yourself what you need right now? Are you mindfully choosing what to do and what not to do?

Your future lies in the choices you make and actions you take today.

principle #5:

accountability

Writing Practice
....
Creating a simulated Wellness Board of Directors

A corporate board of directors is responsible for guiding and overseeing a company's activities and objectives – in other words, for keeping an organization accountable. A wellness board of directors can work in a similar manner, acting as a sounding board, giving encouragement, and providing perspective on your wellness objectives.

Since your board will be fictitious, you have the luxury of selecting anyone your imagination can conjure. You will be holding your board meetings in your notebook, role playing as you provide your status and work through your obstacles.

Try this – Forming and engaging with your board:

- You have the option of having five, seven or twelve board members, with your Future Self as the Chairwoman (and deciding vote).

  - **Five:** Select one person who represents the spirit of each Principle (Self-Compassion,

Intention, Consistency, Growth Mindset, Accountability). For example, for Self-Compassion, you may want to choose the Buddhist nun Pema Chödrön or your grandmother. For Consistency, you may pick a sports figure or your uncle who never missed a day of work. Anyone who appropriately fills this specific role in your life.

- **Seven:** Select one person who represents the spirit of each area on the Holistic Wellness Spectrum (Exercise, Nutrition, Simplify, Energetic Flow, Expression, Spirituality, Relationships). Who exemplifies what you want to aspire to for each area?

- **Twelve:** Combine the people you selected for the Principles and the Holistic Wellness Spectrum areas.

• Set aside an hour of quiet to write in your notebook. Select your board and create your agenda. You may choose to "present" your objective, progress, successes (how you've created accountability for yourself), areas of difficulty (where you'd like to do better next time) and next steps.

• Envision what each board member would have to say about your update. If you didn't achieve your objective, your Consistency board member might have one view, but what would the Self-Compassion member have to offer? If you completed the triathlon you've been training for, your Exercise and Nutrition board members will likely be pleased, but what would be the view of the Relationships member?

- Extra credit: capture screenshots of your wellness board of directors for additional inspiration. You can add the pictures to your digital vision board.

Meditation Practice
R.A.I.N.

Accountability includes taking responsibility and claiming ownership of your actions. This can sometimes bring up difficult emotions when you fall short of your own expectations.

R.A.I.N. is a Buddhist practice used by meditation teachers and popularized by Dr. Tara Brach, author of *True Refuge* and *Radical Compassion* to help work through difficult emotions. It's a simple process that uses the acronym R.A.I.N. for the four steps: Recognize, Allow, Investigate, Nurture.

Try this – R.A.I.N. meditation:

- Whenever a difficult situation or emotion arises, try sitting quietly while going through these four steps:

  - **Recognize what is happening:** Focus your attention on what is happening inside you. What sensations are you feeling? What emotions? Can you name your experience?

- **Allow life to be just as it is:** Acknowledge what is happening without judging, controlling or pushing it away.

- **Investigate with gentle attention:** Explore the physical sensations you're feeling more deeply. For example, if stress is overwhelming, where do you feel it? Tense muscles around your eyes and neck? Is there anger behind the stress? Frustration? Name what you're feeling in detail.

- **Nurture:** Ask yourself what you need most in this moment (e.g., acceptance, protection, hand on heart, deep breath, a walk). Realize the impermanence of the thoughts and emotions you're experiencing. Rest in the knowing that these feelings will shift and this experience does not define or limit you.

Positive Action Practice
Wellness reward system

Rewards are a great way to keep you accountable and having a wellness rewards system adds a little gamification to the equation.

Try this:

- Select an activity that will be rewarded. It can be a goal, an objective, or a series of behaviors (# of days or # of healthy activities over time)

- Develop a list of rewards you enjoy or you find motivating:

  - **Enjoyment rewards:** massage, sleep, spa day, new hairstyle, tattoo, piercing, afternoon in the hammock, artist date

  - **Motivational rewards:** new gear, premium streaming service for workouts, wellness date

  - **Entertainment rewards:** concert, movie, gallery, sports event, comedy club, binge-watching a favorite show

  - **Friendship rewards:** weekend getaway with partner, watching the sunrise, road trip, walk on the beach, picnic, bike ride, star gaze, hike, friends gathering around the firepit or fireplace, volunteering.

- Enjoy the reward and determine the parameters for the next one!

principle #5:
accountability

- Accountability is a powerful determinant of whether or not your wellness intentions will be realized.

- Qualities of accountability can be developed.

- The core tenets of accountability include checking-in, celebrating wins, and making adjustments.

- Three ways to hold yourself accountable are: 1) utilizing tools; 2) finding an accountability partner; and 3) joining a community of interest.

- The choices made and actions taken today will determine your future wellness state.

- In your carry-on:

  - Your Wellness Board of Directors
  - R.A.I.N. practice
  - Wellness reward system

9

sustaining your wellness practices

*Happiness is when what you think, what you say
and what you do are in harmony.*
–Mahatma Gandhi

You are well on your way to prioritizing yourself and
your well-being. By now, you have:

- Read the stories, worked through the Principles,
  and completed the exercises

- Welcomed all of yourself back home with
  compassion

- Determined your motivational "Why" based on
  your beliefs, values and passions

- Consistently found ways to nourish your mind, body and spirit with optimism and enthusiasm
- Created a customized self-care plan that takes into account known barriers
- Developed an accountability support system to help you stay on course.

But how do you integrate your new practices into your life over the long-term and keep your wellness intentions thriving?

Two things have kept me engaged, on-track and productive through the decades: **morning and evening routines** and an **ongoing learning curriculum**.

Morning and Evening Routines

The coffee pot clicks on at 3:45 a.m., fifteen minutes before my morning alarm sounds. I shuffle into the bathroom that glows with the changing images of the digital vision board. By the time I get to the kitchen, sipping a glass of water and giving thanks for the day, I pause to ask myself, "What do I need?" Back in the bedroom with a steaming cup of coffee, I savor the first few sips, mindfully awakening.

While this routine only takes a few minutes, it sets the tone for the day ahead. My morning and evening routines are not tightly structured – sometimes I wake up later, for example – and my actions may change over time. However, I do have certain practices that are always a part of my day: mindfulness, writing, exercise, learning and keeping my home and workspace orderly.

Here's what a typical morning and evening can look like for me:

Example of a Weekday Morning Routine	
4:00am	Quietly begin the day, practicing mindfulness while enjoying a cup of coffee.
4:10am	Begin a 20-minute meditation via a timer, guided meditation, or mindful self-compassion practice.
4:30am	Write in my notebook if I feel the pull or read on a topic of current interest or inspiration.
5:15am	On a gym day, I make the bed and get ready for the session, otherwise I continue with the above.
5:30am	Drive to the gym (or trailhead). The alternative is to run or row in my basement or attend a later CrossFit session.
7:00am	Family time.

Example of a Weekday Evening Routine	
6:00pm	Family time.
7:00pm	Start intermittent fasting (no eating after 7 pm).
8:00pm	Begin to power down, minimizing blue screens (phone, computer, TV); tidy-up the house so it's clean and organized; create a plan for the next day's morning/work.
9:00pm	Wind down the day with loved ones, read, 10-minute meditation before bed.

These are the general guidelines I follow, but they are flexible enough to accommodate life and work events as needed. When my needs and those of my loved ones change, I adjust my schedule accordingly. Also, if I'm working toward something new or need additional positive reinforcement, I may also choose to add visualization and affirmations to my routine for a period of time.

I wasn't always a 4 a.m. riser. The early start to my day came out of necessity during the last few years of my corporate career when I was studying to become a coach and starting my business. In fact, much of this book was written at 4 a.m. before heading off to my "real job." Even though I don't have to get up as early anymore, I find I like getting a jump on the day, especially Monday through Friday.

While I aim for the schedule I outlined above and fulfill that intention most mornings, I have a bare minimum of wellness practices built into each day should I be traveling or enjoying time with loved ones. That minimum includes a five-minute hand-over-heart meditation in the morning, some sort of movement during the day for 30 minutes, and a brief gratitude reflection at bedtime. On those streamlined days, I also try to take periodic mindfulness breaks, such as taking a pause with a few deep breaths or a short walk.

Interestingly enough, the abbreviated routine is how I started my morning and evening practices years ago. But over the years, my practices expanded to provide the support I currently need and enjoy.

I haven't met or read about someone I respect who doesn't have some sort of daily routine, especially in wellness, sports or business. Once I understood that their lives were built deliberately, I began emulating their practices until I found a combination that worked well for me.

Now it's your turn. Since your path to wellness is unique, there is no one right morning or evening routine to recommended. Because practices and routines can vary wildly, you'll want to ask yourself: What will enhance my chance of realizing my wellness intention?

Your daily wellness practices will help you consistently nurture your mind, body and spirit. That, in turn, will give you the energy you need to live the life you envision while remaining grounded each day, especially when things don't go as planned. Your wellness routines should be supportive, not suffocating, nor should they create too rigid a structure.

To get started, here's a template where you can list the time of day you'll begin your wellness routine, the activities you feel will be beneficial, as well as an estimate of the ideal length of the activity.

Daily Routine Template		
Time	Activity	Duration

Here is a menu of potential activities to consider:

- **Silence** – A purposeful break from the nonstop auditory and electronic stimuli to make space and turn attention inward. In the quiet, your mind and nervous system settles so you can listen to your inner wisdom and allow ideas and connections to surface. This process doesn't have to be perfect – dogs bark, traffic continues, kids interrupt. But ask yourself how you can minimize the noise in your life. What are your no phone/computer/TV hours parameters?

- **Meditation/mindfulness** – A practice that contributes to calm, focus and productivity by anchoring awareness in the senses and present moment. The practice can involve formal sitting (mindful self-compassion, lovingkindness, following the breath) or being mindful in everyday activities (eating, walking, driving). Mindfulness practices allow you to feel your body and connect with your inner self-knowing. You'll come to see there is nowhere to be except right where you are.

- **Visualization/affirmations** – These are intended to help create good energy while working toward a new life vision. Visualization is the formation of a mental image and affirmations are positive assertions stated in the present tense. Both help to create and maintain a growth mindset. To use them, revisit your intentions and envision how you will feel once you've achieved that intention. For example, if your intention is to have more physical energy, imagine what you will feel like when you have more vitality. Can you see yourself walking hand in hand with your beloved, running on the beach with your dog, crushing it in the gym? You can also recite reinforcing statements throughout the day, such as "I have plenty of energy to last throughout the day," or "I wake up feeling refreshed and energetic."

- **Journaling** – This is a great way to record your thoughts, feelings and experiences. Writing in your notebook will help you clear your head, process your emotions, and express yourself. Begin each day by asking yourself, "What's going on with me today?" or, in the spirit of mindful self-compassion, "What do I need?" You can also explore worries (What's on my mind, in my heart?), gratitude (What am I thankful for?) and dreams (Where will this lead, how far can I go?). Make a bucket list. The more you write, the deeper you'll go, which can lead to insights, stress management, and coping productively.

- **Making the bed** – This is especially important for those of us who work from home. I make sure to make the bed, shower and dress for the "office," as if I were traveling to work, because, well, I am traveling to work.

- **Inspiration/learning** – Read inspirational passages to stir the heart, take an online class on a topic of interest, or learn all you can about anything related to your intention.

- **Movement** – This includes anything that gets the blood flowing and muscles working. Depending on your exercise goals, you may be looking for physical exertion (running, weight workouts), mind/body connection (yoga, tai chi) or being present with body (walking meditation, time in nature).

- **Simplifying** – A clean, organized life will give you more time, space and energy. When physical and mental clutter are released, you have more capacity to focus on what matters most. Let go of excess baggage and make room for inspiration.

- **Evening routine** – This may include time with your partner and family, preparing for the next day (food, exercise gear, clothes, reviewing your schedule and to do list), cleaning and tidying (dinner dishes, house), and preparing for sleep (unplug, stretch, journal, read).

Ask yourself: what feels doable and sustainable? If you're just starting out, a fifteen-minute routine that includes five minutes of meditation, a few minutes of affirmations and jotting down three things you're grateful for in your notebook each morning may be enough. Experiment to find what feels right and works best for you.

It will take time to settle on a supportive routine. After trying your initial sequence for a few weeks, revisit the process in your notebook and make any changes. And remember the most important thing is consistency!

For the longer term, plan to revisit your morning and evening routines periodically, especially when your life circumstances change, your wellness practices increase, or your intentions are modified.

Above all, your routine should help you stay on track with your heart's desires.

Your Curriculum –
Ongoing Self-Directed Learning

While your morning and evening routines provide a sustaining structure for your wellness practices, an ongoing learning program will help keep you interested and your wellness routines fresh.

As an added bonus, researchers have shown that learning can change our brain chemistry for the better by improving cognitive connections and adaptability to change. In addition, learning deepens our understanding of different subject matters, helping us to stay relevant and engaged.

Learning new things about interesting topics also fuels enthusiasm, especially if you build this learning into your everyday life. Daily learning keeps you curious and can lead you outside of your comfort zone (where the magic happens) to an overall richer, more creative life experience.

If you analyze your current work and personal interests, you'll most likely identify many areas where you are learning new things. You can draw on the pool of knowledge you've already amassed along with any training opportunities you may have in your day to day.

When I was in the corporate world, I used to look at my stocked bookshelves in my home and dream of taking a year-long, self-imposed sabbatical and creating my own curriculum of learning.

Now as a writer and a coach, I get to spend my days learning about topics I love. But looking back I can see I've been a life-long learner.

For example, during my corporate career, I had the opportunity to learn every day through assignments, travel, on-the-job training, continuing education, presentations, mentoring or teaching. At the time I had no idea how important it would be to know about business models, strategic planning, sales and marketing, operations, return on investment, risk management, communication, negotiation and meeting facilitation as an entrepreneur.

Concurrently, and without even realizing it, I created my own system of learning beyond business topics. I always had a book (later iPad) and highlighter in hand, taking copious notes during my work commute, on planes, and during my morning or evening routines.

The topics I was interested in ranged from music (favorite bands, playing guitar, songwriting, audio engineering, forming a band, playing a gig), to creativity (favorite books, learning to write, writing creative non-fiction, photography) to wellness (nutrition for enhanced wellness, food preparation, exercise fundamentals, meditation, mindful self-compassion, spirituality, minimalism), to fitness (running, marathon training, ultra-running, cycling, weight training), to entrepreneurship (starting a business, coaching) – to name a few!

My love of learning also extended beyond books to lectures, classes, online learning, workshops and retreats. Learning was a great way to meet and spend time with experts, while networking with others and creating community and accountability.

"Take inventory of your professional and personal interests and opportunities for further learning. Not only can you use the knowledge to enhance your wellness practices, but the act of learning itself may lead to better health, emotional resilience, and cognition."

Take inventory of your professional and personal interests and opportunities for further learning. Not only can you use the knowledge to enhance your wellness practices, but the act of learning itself may lead to better health, emotional resilience, and cognition.

As you've worked through the exercises in this book and spent time writing in your notebook, what topics of interest have emerged for you? Where would you like to expand your learning? Perhaps you'd like to go deeper on a subject you already love, or explore a completely new area. Is there a skillset you'd like to build?

We are living in a time where we have unprecedented access to information and can learn about anything we wish. This provides a number of viable options to create a self-directed learning program:

- **Reading** – books, blogs, online publishing platforms, like Medium

- **Viewing** – educational videos, online courses, TED talks

- **Listening** – podcasts, audiobooks

- **Formal/group training** – local college, community adult classes, workshops, retreats)

- **Informal training** – mentor, coach

- **Learning by doing** – Toastmasters, blogging

- **Emulating your mentors** – books, classes, deconstructing their approach

- **Teaching what you learn** – professional organizations, volunteering

- **Discussion/feedback groups** – in person, online.

Once you find a topic(s) of interest and suitable learning methods, you can easily structure your learning as follows:

- **Instruction** – as noted above
- **Practice** – experimenting and performing the new skill
- **Community** – sharing it publicly and getting feedback
- **Repetition** – learning from the process, incorporating the feedback and trying again.

Advantages of using a framework like this is that there is little to no cost and you get to share publicly in a low stakes manner. For example, you can volunteer to give a talk at a local Rotary Club or write an article on a favorite topic to share what you've learned.

How you design your learning is up to you. You can create a plan that is completely unstructured (just a topic) or defined to include goals, timelines, progress measures and completion targets. You can proactively grow your skillset in your own unique way.

Self-improvement is an investment in yourself and will keep you motivated. Experiment and amend your practices as you continue to learn and grow.

chapter **10**

reconnection = optimized well-being

*"The cave you fear to enter
holds the treasure you seek."*
–Joseph Campbell

Congratulations on choosing to reconnect with your full self in order to live a more empowered and wholehearted life!

- You dared to imagine what it would feel like to bring your whole self to work, life and play.

- You had the courage to listen to and act on your inner voice, integrating your shadow self and forging a new relationship with yourself.

- You acknowledged that there are no shortcuts to learning and practicing new ways of being.

- You chose to take steps to make the best optimized wellness choices.

- You committed to embracing growth.

- You repurposed your time and made your own self-care non-negotiable.

- You expressed what's in your heart because you know you are worth it.

- You embodied *The Athena Principles* by working toward what you really want in life, which empowered you and inspired others.

I invite you to revisit the "Perfect Day" exercise you did in Chapter Three. Does that vision still hold true? Are you dreaming bigger? Feel free to update as needed.

Wellness transformation is like a slow-motion chain reaction. When you find ways to reconnect with yourself, you make better wellness choices to support the aim to live more wholeheartedly. That, in turn, leads to optimized well-being. Again and again, in the thousands of decisions you make each day, you will become more aligned with your deepest desires.

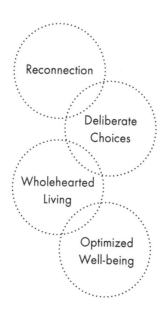

As you move closer toward your true desires, the feeling of disconnect from your true self will fade in your rearview mirror. You'll no longer need to live with the feeling of having a low-grade fever (fragmented, empty, isolated, stuck, unfulfilled, apathetic, fatigued, depleted) or with more intense feelings like overwhelm, frustration, sadness, anger or despair.

As you experience wholeheartedness, you'll become better at dealing with the source of the disconnect, such as office environments, relationship expectations, societal norms, over-commitment, busyness or anything that requires you to hide, mask or numb your true self.

As you continue to move toward living authentically, how do you navigate the tension between who you are in the world today and what you feel in your heart? The initial discomfort you may feel as you move forward toward wholeheartedness is stuck energy getting unstuck. The older that stuck energy is, the harder it can be to dislodge.

In addition, it can be difficult to switch back and forth from your current life circumstances to deliberate actions that move you closer to your desires. That's why so many people abandon their dreams in exchange for a life that fits in with their family and friends. But you play small when you minimize what resonates deeply within yourself.

By reclaiming your wholeness, you step into your personal power; that is, you embrace your whole self with pride, without needing to compartmentalize parts of yourself that once felt unworthy.

It takes energy to protect the unspoken and unexpressed sides of yourself in order to fit in. Letting go of things that keep you stuck and unhappy, things that no longer serve – allows you to make space for what you desire. The result is a more authentic presence and the newfound energy leads to greater productivity.

Once you get a foothold on that space, you'll need to protect it from the noise of daily living. A good way to honor that space is to become aware of it and be present in that pause. It will also serve you to create containers of time for activities (email, news, catch-up administration) that tend to siphon off your solo time.

By prioritizing this quality time with yourself, your daily actions will come from a place of deliberateness and calmness instead of from autopilot. Becoming aware of what you feed your mind, body and spirit will tip the scale from doing to being and life itself will become your practice. At that point, you will have created a calm space in which to grow curiosity, enjoyment, appreciation, contemplation, connection and inner exploration.

Back in Chapter Two we introduced the Holistic Wellness Spectrum as a tool to find entry points to increased wellness. Using the three main categories of the inventory (Vitality, Flow and Connection), here are some techniques to help you stay connected with yourself and your personal power.

Holistic Wellness Spectrum

Vitality

- Ask yourself, "What do I need," and either give what you need to yourself or create an action plan to move toward it

- Let go of perfection

- Move out of your comfort zone by taking measured risks

- Avoid numbing out (e.g., eating, drinking, tech, TV, overscheduling)

- Move your body every day in some way

- Eat mindfully and, periodically, in silence

- Create a recovery protocol that includes sound sleep habits

Holistic Wellness Spectrum

VITALITY		FLOW			CONNECTION	
Exercise & Nutrition		*Simplifying, Energetic Flow & Expression*			*Spirituality & Relationships*	
MOVE	NOURISH	SIMPLIFY	FLOW	CREATE	CONTEMPLATE	CONNECT
· Train	· Clean Nutrition	· Let Go	· Presence	· Expression	· Spirituality	· Intimate Relationship
· Aerobic	· Plant-based	· Possessions	· Intention	· Ideas	· Inner Work	· Family
· Strength	· Paleo/Keto/ Zone	· People	· Discernment	· Visual Art	· Reflection	· Friends
· Functional	· Hybrid	· Ways of Being	· Deliberate Action	· Writing	· Lovingkindness	· Aligned Tribe
· Stretch/Roll	· Hydrate	· Empty Space	· Intuitive Living	· Music	· Compassion	· Holding Space/ Depth
· Massage	· Supplement	· Mindful Consumption	· Own Rhythm	· Acting/Dance	· Generosity	· Empathy
· Recover	· Blended Meals	· Tech Detox	· Ease	· Explore	· Gratitude	· Support
· Sleep	· Intermittent Fasting	· Surroundings That Reflect Current Self	· Heartful	· Inspire	· Ritual	· Mentor
· Physical Health	· Wild/Local Food		· Positive Mindset	· Purpose	· Quest	· Social Circle
· Energy Management	· Healthy Recipes	· Morning/Evening Routines	· Financial Health	· Impact	· Nature	· Celebration
· Stress Management	· Food Preperation		· Volunteer	· Aligned Livelihood	· Listen	· Fun/Play
· Self-care	· Systems/Support			· Ongoing Learning	· Meditate	· Adventure
					· Rejuvinate	
					· Legacy	

- Create a self-care protocol that includes ways to minimize impact to your energy levels and managing stress
- Stick to the basics - don't overcomplicate healthy living (you may simply need to eat less and move more) and make your new routine fun

Flow

- Simplify your living environment
- Scale back and slow down your schedule to make room for morning and evening routines
- Say "No" as a way to give yourself permission to prioritize your life and desires. To quote writer Anne Lamott, "No is a complete sentence."
- Let go of anything or anyone who does not support the realization of your dreams
- Schedule time to be on your devices and blocks of time when you are disconnected
- Treat your belongings and resources respectfully
- Dress in a way that makes you feel good
- Create anything – write, paint, collage, take photographs, dance, create a self-portrait
- Schedule "me" time in the form of a wellness or artist date, a new experience or doing what lights you up
- Invest in learning
- Dream big and create an action plan to make it happen

Connection

- Practice self-love and lovingkindness and compassion each day by yourself or with your partner
- Connect with a larger force (participate in a spiritual practice, such as meditation, ritual, gratitude, being in nature)
- Create and spend time in an intentional or sanctuary space
- Be of service
- Keep connected with your partner, family, friends and community, fully showing up (sharing your true thoughts and desires)
- Welcome and seek out new experiences
- Play and laugh
- Step outside yourself and your comfort zone
- Plan a road trip or travel to a new destination

Wellness is a lifestyle – a way of living that incorporates nourishing and replenishing behaviors that contribute to your growth and well-being. A way of allowing your mind, body and spirit to integrate and use its universal wisdom to keep you vibrant.

But the journey doesn't end here, in fact, it's just beginning. Taking action to live your life as you define it is your ultimate act of power. May you fall in love with taking care of yourself.

Be well – the best is yet to come!

epilogue

"Traveler, there is no path. The path is made by walking. By walking you make a path."
-Antonio Machado

When I crossed the ultramarathon finish line at 54, I was not the same person who had begun working out two decades prior. When I was 35, I defined wellness in terms of diet and exercise and looked for a pre-packaged solution to enhance my wellness.

Now, at midlife, I know from 20 years of personal research and experimentation that wellness includes so much more than nutrition and movement, and no one can provide the wellness solution that's right for me. I have to do that for myself. I also have the benefit of hindsight to help me see how I carved out my own path to wellness.

- I put down my superwoman cape of overachievement and perfectionism and accepted all aspects of myself.

- I found my still point so I could listen to my inner wisdom for guidance.

- I redirected time that was not moving me forward and invested it in more productive activities, starting with five minutes at a time.

- I stepped out of my comfort zone in each of the wellness areas in order to continue learning and growing.

- I let go of anything or anyone that didn't support my vision of living a wholehearted life.

- I applied *The Athena Principles* methodology and practices repeatedly in all categories of the Holistic Wellness Spectrum.

- I trusted the next step would be revealed when I plateaued or the path was not visible.

I may have started this journey with a focus on diet and exercise, but as I moved forward, I found a heart-centered way of living focused on feeding the good wolf inside of me. I found myself and my purpose, and began working with people in the middle of their own midlife journey who were looking to transform their lives. I found a fun, enthusiastic and growth-minded tribe of friends around the globe.

It's a privilege to be on this journey with you. May you continue to honor yourself by embracing wellness as a vital and ongoing process of making choices to create a healthy, integrated and fulfilling life.

Appendix

Resources

A free companion Athena Principles workbook is available for download at www.AthenaWellness.com.

References

Chapter	Page	Reference
1	30	David Whyte, davidwhyte.com
2, 8	45, 165	Cycle for the Cause, cycleforthecause.org
3	55, 202	Self as the Source of the Story, Christina Baldwin, peerspirit.com
4, 9	88, 183	Mindful Self-Compassion, centerformsc.org
5	102	Danielle LaPorte, daniellelaporte.com
5	111	*The Artist's Way*, Julia Cameron, juliacameronlive.com
6	119	Tony Horton, tonyhortonlife.com
6	133	Future Self Visualization, coactive.com
7	149	Thich Nhat Hanh, plumvillage.org
8	169	Tara Brach, tarabrach.com

Acknowledgements

Teachers/mentors that have blessed my life, sparked inspiration, and have been shining examples pointing the way – their generosity of time and advice can never be repaid.

Writing

- Christina Baldwin, whose Self as the Source of the Story circle of courageous women in June 2009 expertly stripped away that tough Jersey girl exterior to reveal the tender place where writing is born. Turns out, it's also an excellent place from which to live and love.

- Laurie Wagner, Maya Stein and the gals in the No Boundaries and Wild Writing circles who strengthen me through their vulnerable storytelling and floor me with their breathtaking prose.

- Jen Louden for the practical approach and advice during our Colorado retreat and the "You Are Awesome" gals who continue to support and encourage.

Business

- Colleagues throughout my 33-year corporate career who were committed to conducting business at the highest standards and to making an impact by supporting diversity and contributing time and resources to those underserved. I deeply appreciate our conversations and your ongoing support as I venture into uncharted waters.

Wellness

- Amanda Cook, who coached me as I shaped Athena Wellness into a viable enterprise with her heart-based business guidance and continued friendship.

- Beth Hale, who helped turn my Athena Wellness vision into a beautifully designed, web-based reality.

- Brad and Susannah Cooper at Catalyst Coaching Institute for their training and support throughout the wellness coach certification process.

- Rich Roll, who inspired me to run my first marathon and ultramarathon after reading his book, *Finding Ultra* – and whose encouragement during the PlantPower Italia retreat reinforced my determination to take the leap into serving others through wellness offerings.

- Dorie Clark, whose books, blogs and in-person strategy session set me on my way to entrepreneurial success.

- My first coaching clients and workshop participants who trusted me early in my coaching and teaching career.

Editors/book production – Yes, it takes a village to bring a book into the world and I've come to learn that writing the manuscript is the easy part. Many thanks to:

- Shari Caudron, a developmental editorial partnership born out of the best Google search ever. You have shaped this book into something I'm proud of and have become a trusted colleague in the process – this writer cannot find suitable words to sufficiently thank you.

- Laurie Wagner, who gave me feedback on the writing exercises and has taught me the importance of leading with vulnerability when holding space for writers.

- Early readers Kristie McLean and Kathy Koop who provided initial feedback and encouragement and were the first to say I was developing something worthwhile.

- Anna Bourne, Gerry Dixon and Deon Minnaar, who taught me the importance of excellent client service and offered inspiration and support early in the journey through their stories and experiences.

- Beta readers Denise Thomson, Kristin Walle and Kerrie MacPherson, overworked professionals themselves, whose willingness to devote time from their busy lives to provide detailed and astute feedback is greatly appreciated.

- Liz Kalloch, whose amazing design talent graces the cover and inside of this book to make it a beautiful read.

- Amy Tingle, who brought great comfort in one final review with her keen proofreading.

- Sarah Flannery, for the beautiful photos and ease with which they were taken.

- ListenUp Audiobooks for their superb audiobook assistance.

- Steve Weiss, who provided the Athena inspiration through his exquisite tales.

My "Framily" (friends as family)

- My mommas at TNT Fitness: Tiffani Hill (The Original Momma), Ro Aquila (Marylou), Janet Perusini (Smiling Momma and libation engineer) and Dee Finamore-Jones (Momma Dee).

- Denise Miccoli, Steven Grant and all my new friends at Mahwah CrossFit – the box with heart *and* badass athletes.

- The Rich Roll PlantPower Italia 2019 retreaters – we experienced some amazing and intense things together in the hills of Tuscany.

- My BFFs: Kristie, Denise and Kristin – always a phone call away, thank you; Artie Bergman who turned my home into a haven (and home office); Ann Lee for 25+ years of haircuts, conversation and connection; and Jan Siegmund, who continues to inspire with his age-defying athletic pursuits.

Family – my Irish and Italian famiglia

- Dad, 98-years-young and ahead of his time in terms of wellness and positive mindset.

- Mom, grandma and all the family and friends who are no longer with us but their presence is felt daily and their legacies continue to impact.

- Siblings Richie and Eileen and their families: Priscilla, Steve, Sarah-Jane & Paul, Stella & Aurora, Mark & Mark, Christopher & Kim, Jason & Ali – I'm blessed to be a part of your lives.

About the Author

Prior to becoming a certified wellness coach, workshop leader and author, Kathy Robinson spent more than 25 years assessing the wellness of Fortune 500 companies. She was a Chief Audit Executive and Chief Risk Officer before turning the lens from professional assessments to personal ones and began helping her individual clients optimize their well-being, especially in times of transition or when striving toward new wellness goals. She also teaches and consults with companies committed to enhancing the wellness of their employees.

Kathy practices what she preaches and is passionate about wellness, nutrition and exercise. She believes that a positive attitude is the accelerator that propels us through transformation. You can find her at the local CrossFit box and running the trails in northern New Jersey, where she completed her first marathon and ultramarathon at age 54.

www.AthenaWellness.com